W9-ANA-596

Modern Critical Interpretations

Jane Austen's
Pride and Prejudice

Modern Critical Interpretations

The Oresteia
Beowulf
The General Prologue to The Canterbury Tales
The Pardoner's Tale
The Knight's Tale
The Divine Comedy
Exodus
Genesis
The Gospels
The Iliad
The Book of Job
Volpone
Doctor Faustus
The Revelation of St. John the Divine
The Song of Songs
Oedipus Rex
The Aeneid
The Duchess of Malfi
Antony and Cleopatra
As You Like It
Coriolanus
Hamlet
Henry IV, Part I
Henry IV, Part II
Henry V
Julius Caesar
King Lear
Macbeth
Measure for Measure
The Merchant of Venice
A Midsummer Night's Dream
Much Ado About Nothing
Othello
Richard II
Richard III
The Sonnets
Taming of the Shrew
The Tempest
Twelfth Night
The Winter's Tale
Emma
Mansfield Park
Pride and Prejudice
The Life of Samuel Johnson
Moll Flanders
Robinson Crusoe
Tom Jones
The Beggar's Opera
Gray's Elegy
Paradise Lost
The Rape of the Lock
Tristram Shandy
Gulliver's Travels

Evelina
The Marriage of Heaven and Hell
Songs of Innocence and Experience
Jane Eyre
Wuthering Heights
Don Juan
The Rime of the Ancient Mariner
Bleak House
David Copperfield
Hard Times
A Tale of Two Cities
Middlemarch
The Mill on the Floss
Jude the Obscure
The Mayor of Casterbridge
The Return of the Native
Tess of the D'Urbervilles
The Odes of Keats
Frankenstein
Vanity Fair
Barchester Towers
The Prelude
The Red Badge of Courage
The Scarlet Letter
The Ambassadors
Daisy Miller, The Turn of the Screw, and Other Tales
The Portrait of a Lady
Billy Budd, Benito Cereno, Bartleby the Scrivener, and Other Tales
Moby-Dick
The Tales of Poe
Walden
Adventures of Huckleberry Finn
The Life of Frederick Douglass
Heart of Darkness
Lord Jim
Nostromo
A Passage to India
Dubliners
A Portrait of the Artist as a Young Man
Ulysses
Kim
The Rainbow
Sons and Lovers
Women in Love
1984
Major Barbara

Man and Superman
Pygmalion
St. Joan
The Playboy of the Western World
The Importance of Being Earnest
Mrs. Dalloway
To the Lighthouse
My Antonia
An American Tragedy
Murder in the Cathedral
The Waste Land
Absalom, Absalom!
Light in August
Sanctuary
The Sound and the Fury
The Great Gatsby
A Farewell to Arms
The Sun Also Rises
Arrowsmith
Lolita
The Iceman Cometh
Long Day's Journey Into Night
The Grapes of Wrath
Miss Lonelyhearts
The Glass Menagerie
A Streetcar Named Desire
Their Eyes Were Watching God
Native Son
Waiting for Godot
Herzog
All My Sons
Death of a Salesman
Gravity's Rainbow
All the King's Men
The Left Hand of Darkness
The Brothers Karamazov
Crime and Punishment
Madame Bovary
The Interpretation of Dreams
The Castle
The Metamorphosis
The Trial
Man's Fate
The Magic Mountain
Montaigne's Essays
Remembrance of Things Past
The Red and the Black
Anna Karenina
War and Peace

These and other titles in preparation

Jane Austen's
Pride and Prejudice

Edited and with an introduction by

Harold Bloom
Sterling Professor of the Humanities
Yale University

Chelsea House Publishers
NEW YORK ◇ PHILADELPHIA

© 1987 by Chelsea House Publishers, a division
of Main Line Book Co.

5   7   9   8   6

Introduction © 1987 by Harold Bloom

Printed and bound in the United States of America

∞ The paper used in this publication meets the minimum requirements
of the American National Standard for Permanence of Paper for Printed
Library Materials, Z39.48 –1984.

Library of Congress Cataloging-in-Publication Data
Jane Austen's Pride and prejudice.
    (Modern critical interpretations)
    Bibliography: p.
    Includes index.
    Summary: Eight selections of literary criticism on a classic comedy of
manners.
    1. Austen, Jane, 1775–1817. Pride and prejudice.   [1. Austen,
Jane, 1775–1817. Pride and prejudice.   2. English literature — History
and criticism]
I. Bloom, Harold.   II. Series.
PR4034.P72J36   1986   823'.7   86 –17152
ISBN   0–87754–945–1

Contents

Editor's Note

This book brings together a representative selection of the best criticism that has been devoted to Jane Austen's *Pride and Prejudice*, reprinted here in the chronological order of its original publication. I am grateful to Susan Laity for her erudition and judgment in helping to locate and choose these critical essays.

The introduction traces Elizabeth Bennet's descent, as a heroine of the Protestant will, from Richardson's Clarissa Harlowe and finds in both figures the Puritan passion to confer and subsequently accept esteem as an ultimate power of the individual soul. Jane Nardin begins the chronological sequence with an investigation of the close relation between manners and moral character in *Pride and Prejudice*, a relation that assumes an almost Platonic correspondence between convention and virtue. Akin to this correspondence is the dialectic that Stuart M. Tave uncovers between affection and the "amiable" man, where the parodistic sense of what it means to be "amiable" is transcended by a better sense, almost beyond the reach of irony.

Erotic transference in an educational context is Juliet McMaster's emphasis in her study of "love and pedagogy," which charmingly ends with a vision of Elizabeth perpetually learning tact from Darcy, and Darcy in turn learning always how to be laughed at, from and by Elizabeth. Gene W. Ruoff briefly but sharply analyzes *Pride and Prejudice* as two works interleaved, a novel of action, and a novel of feeling in which personal maturation frequently has an inverse relation to what happens. Elizabeth Bennet's maturation, which is accomplished both despite her parents' "anarchic energies of cynicism and insensibility," and because of her resistance to those energies, is the emphasis in Julia Prewitt Brown's study of Austen's "authorial voice." The larger relation of the novel's structure to Austen's social vision is described by David Monaghan as a true marriage of form and content, so that the narrative itself becomes a metaphor for the order and harmony that Austen desires and celebrates.

Susan Morgan, asserting that "Elizabeth's freedom is basically the freedom to think for herself," finds in both author and heroine the image of an intelligence that learns to accept clarity as an evolving achievement, revelation as an extended process in time. In this volume's final essay, Jan Fergus shows *Pride and Prejudice* to be the apotheosis of the comedy of manners, and so to constitute a grand advance upon novels even as accomplished as Burney's *Evelina* and Richardson's *Sir Charles Grandison*. Just as the editor's introduction found in Elizabeth Bennet a heroism of the Protestant will, modulated from tragedy into high comedy, so the final study here discovers in *Pride and Prejudice* the modulation of a literary convention from a restraint into a resource.

Introduction

The oddest yet by no means inapt analogy to Jane Austen's art of representation is Shakespeare's — oddest, because she is so careful of limits, as classical as Ben Jonson in that regard, and Shakespeare transcends all limits. Austen's humor, her mode of rhetorical irony, is not particularly Shakespearean, and yet her precision and accuracy of representation is. Like Shakespeare, she gives us figures, major and minor, utterly consistent each in her or his own mode of speech and being, and utterly different from one another. Her heroines have firm selves, each molded with an individuality that continues to suggest Austen's reserve of power, her potential for creating an endless diversity. To recur to the metaphor of oddness, the highly deliberate limitation of social scale in Austen seems a paradoxical theater of mind in which so fecund a humanity could be fostered. Irony, the concern of most critics of Austen, seems more than a trope in her work, seems indeed to be the condition of her language, yet hardly accounts for the effect of moral and spiritual power that she so constantly conveys, however implicitly or obliquely.

Ian Watt, in his permanently useful *The Rise of the Novel*, portrays Austen as Fanny Burney's direct heir in the difficult art of combining the rival modes of Samuel Richardson and Henry Fielding. Like Burney, Austen is thus seen as following the Richardson of *Sir Charles Grandison*, in a "minute presentation of daily life," while emulating Fielding in "adopting a more detached attitude to her narrative material, and in evaluating it from a comic and objective point of view." Watt goes further when he points out that Austen tells her stories in a discreet variant of Fielding's manner "as a confessed author," though her ironical juxtapositions are made to appear not those of "an intrusive author but rather of some august and impersonal spirit of social and psychological understanding."

And yet, as Watt knows, Austen truly is the daughter of Richardson, and not of Fielding, just as she is the ancestor of George Eliot and Henry James, rather than of Dickens and Thackeray. Her inwardness is an ironic revision of Richardson's extraordinary conversion of English Protestant sensibility into the

1

figure of Clarissa Harlowe, and her own moral and spiritual concerns fuse in the crucial need of her heroines to sustain their individual integrities, a need so intense that it compels them to fall into those errors about life that are necessary for life (to adopt a Nietzschean formulation). In this too they follow, though in a comic register, the pattern of their tragic precursor, the magnificent but sublimely flawed Clarissa Harlowe.

Richardson's *Clarissa*, perhaps still the longest novel in the language, seems to me also still the greatest, despite the achievements of Austen, Dickens, George Eliot, Henry James, and Joyce. Austen's Elizabeth Bennet and Emma Woodhouse, Eliot's Dorothea Brooke and Gwendolen Harleth, James's Isabel Archer and Milly Theale — though all these are Clarissa Harlowe's direct descendants, they are not proportioned to her more sublime scale. David Copperfield and Leopold Bloom have her completeness; indeed Joyce's Bloom may be the most complete representation of a human being in all of literature. But they belong to the secular age; Clarissa Harlowe is poised upon the threshold that leads from the Protestant religion to a purely secular sainthood.

C. S. Lewis, who read Milton as though that fiercest of Protestant temperaments had been an orthodox Anglican, also seems to have read Jane Austen by listening for her echoings of the New Testament. Quite explicitly, Lewis named Austen as the daughter of Dr. Samuel Johnson, greatest of literary critics, and rigorous Christian moralist:

> I feel . . . sure that she is the daughter of Dr. Johnson: she inherits
> his commonsense, his morality, even much of his style.

The Johnson of *Rasselas* and of *The Rambler*, surely the essential Johnson, is something of a classical ironist, but we do not read Johnson for his ironies, or for his dramatic representations of fictive selves. Rather, we read him as we read Koheleth; he writes wisdom literature. That Jane Austen is a wise writer is indisputable, but we do not read *Pride and Prejudice* as though it were Ecclesiastes. Doubtless, Austen's religious ideas were as profound as Samuel Richardson's were shallow, but *Emma* and *Clarissa* are Protestant novels without being in any way religious. What is most original about the representation of Clarissa Harlowe is the magnificent intensity of her slowly described dying, which goes on for about the last third of Richardson's vast novel, in a Puritan ritual that celebrates the preternatural strength of her will. For that is Richardson's sublime concern: the self-reliant apotheosis of the Protestant will. What is tragedy in *Clarissa* becomes serious or moral comedy in *Pride and Prejudice* and *Emma*, and something just the other side of comedy in *Mansfield Park* and *Persuasion*.

II

Rereading *Pride and Prejudice* gives one a sense of Proustian ballet beautifully working itself through in the novel's formal centerpiece, the deferred but progressive mutual enlightenment of Elizabeth and Darcy in regard to the other's true nature. "Proper pride" is what they learn to recognize in one another; propriety scarcely needs definition in that phrase, but precisely what is the pride that allows amiability to flourish? Whatever it is in Darcy, to what extent is it an art of the will in Elizabeth Bennet? Consider the superb scene of Darcy's first and failed marriage proposal:

> While settling this point, she was suddenly roused by the sound of the door-bell, and her spirits were a little fluttered by the idea of its being Colonel Fitzwilliam himself, who had once before called late in the evening, and might now come to inquire particularly after her. But this idea was soon banished, and her spirits were very differently affected, when, to her utter amazement, she saw Mr. Darcy walk into the room. In an hurried manner he immediately began an inquiry after her health, imputing his visit to a wish of hearing that she were better. She answered him with cold civility. He sat down for a few moments, and then getting up, walked about the room. Elizabeth was surprised, but said not a word. After a silence of several minutes, he came towards her in an agitated manner, and thus began:
>
> "In vain have I struggled. It will not do. My feelings will not be repressed. You must allow me to tell you how ardently I admire and love you."
>
> Elizabeth's astonishment was beyond expression. She stared, coloured, doubted, and was silent. This he considered sufficient encouragement; and the avowal of all that he felt, and had long felt for her, immediately followed. He spoke well; but there were feelings besides those of the heart to be detailed, and he was not more eloquent on the subject of tenderness than of pride. His sense of her inferiority—of its being a degradation—of the family obstacles which judgment had always opposed to inclination, were dwelt on with a warmth which seemed due to the consequence he was wounding, but was very unlikely to recommend his suit.
>
> In spite of her deeply-rooted dislike, she could not be insensible to the compliment of such a man's affection, and though her intentions did not vary for an instant, she was at first sorry for the pain he was to receive; till, roused to resentment by his subsequent language, she

lost all compassion in anger. She tried, however, to compose herself to answer him with patience, when he should have done. He concluded with representing to her the strength of that attachment which, in spite of all his endeavours, he had found impossible to conquer; and with expressing his hope that it would now be rewarded by her acceptance of his hand. As he said this, she could easily see that he had no doubt of a favourable answer. He *spoke* of apprehension and anxiety, but his countenance expressed real security. Such a circumstance could only exasperate farther, and, when he ceased, the colour rose into her cheeks, and she said:

"In such cases as this, it is, I believe, the established mode to express a sense of obligation for the sentiments avowed, however unequally they may be returned. It is natural that obligation should be felt, and if I could *feel* gratitude, I would now thank you. But I cannot — I have never desired your good opinion, and you have certainly bestowed it most unwillingly. I am sorry to have occasioned pain to anyone. It has been most unconsciously done, however, and I hope will be of short duration. The feelings which, you tell me, have long prevented the acknowledgment of your regard, can have little difficulty in overcoming it after this explanation."

Mr. Darcy, who was leaning against the mantelpiece with his eyes fixed on her face, seemed to catch her words with no less resentment than surprise. His complexion became pale with anger, and the disturbance of his mind was visible in every feature. He was struggling for the appearance of composure, and would not open his lips till he believed himself to have attained it. The pause was to Elizabeth's feelings dreadful. At length, in a voice of forced calmness, he said:

"And this is all the reply which I am to have the honour of expecting! I might, perhaps, wish to be informed why, with so little *endeavour* at civility, I am thus rejected. But it is of small importance."

Stuart M. Tave believes that both Darcy and Elizabeth become so changed by one another that their "happiness is deserved by a process of mortification begun early and ended late," mortification here being the wounding of pride. Tave's learning and insight are impressive, but I favor the judgment that Elizabeth and Darcy scarcely change, and learn rather that they complement each other's not wholly illegitimate pride. They come to see that their wills are naturally allied, since they have no differences upon the will. The will to what? Their will, Austen's, is neither the will to live nor the will to power. They wish to be esteemed precisely where they estimate value to be high, and neither can afford to make a fundamental error, which is both the anxiety and the comedy of the first proposal scene. Why after all does Darcy allow himself to be eloquent on the subject of his pride, to the extraordinary extent of conveying "with a warmth" what Austen grimly names as "his sense of her inferiority"?

As readers, we have learned already that Elizabeth is inferior to no one, whoever he is. Indeed, I sense as the novel closes (though nearly all Austen critics, and doubtless Austen herself, would disagree with me) that Darcy is her inferior, amiable and properly prideful as he is. I do not mean by this that Elizabeth is a clearer representation of Austenian values than Darcy ever could be; that is made finely obvious by Austen, and her critics have developed her ironic apprehension, which is that Elizabeth incarnates the standard of measurement in her cosmos. There is also a transcendent strength to Elizabeth's will that raises her above that cosmos, in a mode that returns us to Clarissa Harlowe's transcendence of her society, of Lovelace, and even of everything in herself that is not the will to a self-esteem that has also made an accurate estimate of every other will to pride it ever has encountered.

I am suggesting that Ralph Waldo Emerson (who to me is sacred) was mistaken when he rejected Austen as a "sterile" upholder of social conformities and social ironies, as an author who could not celebrate the soul's freedom from societal conventions. Austen's ultimate irony is that Elizabeth Bennet is inwardly so free that convention performs for her the ideal function it cannot perform for us: it liberates her will without tending to stifle her high individuality. But we ought to be wary of even the most distinguished of Austen's moral celebrants, Lionel Trilling, who in effect defended her against Emerson by seeing *Pride and Prejudice* as a triumph "of morality as style." If Emerson wanted to see a touch more Margaret Fuller in Elizabeth Bennet (sublimely ghastly notion!), Trilling wanted to forget the Emersonian law of Compensation, which is that nothing is got for nothing:

> The relation of Elizabeth Bennet to Darcy is real, is intense, but it expresses itself as a conflict and reconciliation of styles: a formal rhetoric, traditional and rigorous, must find a way to accomodate a female vivacity, which in turn must recognize the principled demands of the strict male syntax. The high moral import of the novel lies in the fact that the union of styles is accomplished without injury to either lover.

Yes and no, I would say. Yes, because the wills of both lovers work by similar dialectics, but also no, because Elizabeth's will is more intense and purer, and inevitably must be dimmed by her dwindling into a wife, even though Darcy may well be the best man that society could offer to her. Her pride has playfulness in it, a touch even of the Quixotic. Uncannily, she is both her father's daughter and Samuel Richardson's daughter as well. Her wit is Mr. Bennet's, refined and elaborated, but her will, and her pride in her will, returns us to Clarissa's Puritan passion to maintain the power of the self to confer esteem, and to accept esteem only in response to its bestowal.

Propriety as a Test of Character: *Pride and Prejudice*

Jane Nardin

In *Pride and Prejudice*, Jane Austen makes the basic assumption that a person's out-ward manners mirror his moral character. If, in this novel, a man or woman always displays good manners, it is perfectly safe for the reader to assume that his character is truly good. The characters in the novel continually try to evaluate one another's manners and the moral worth to which they are a clue. Often these evaluations are wrong, but it is important to note that they are never wrong because the manners of the individual in question have lied about his character. If an attempt to judge character from manners backfires in the world of *Pride and Prejudice*, it is invariably either because the judging individual has misperceived the nature of the manners of the individual he is judging, or because the standard of propriety according to which the judgment is being made is a mistaken one. The problem of judgment in *Pride and Prejudice* is not, as it is in *Persuasion*, for ex-ample, primarily a question of penetrating behind the facade of the manners to the reality of moral character; rather it is a question of perceiving and estimating the nature of an individual's manners with a reasonable degree of accuracy.

In a novel where a person's public manners are assumed to be an accurate clue to his private character, the definition of what truly proper manners actually are has an extraordinary importance. The reader must be convinced that the stan-dard of propriety in question is one to which intelligent people of good feeling can give their wholehearted adherence. Jane Austen, it seems to me, achieves this aim in *Pride and Prejudice*. Elizabeth Bennet's standards of decorous behavior do not grate upon the reader's sensibilities as, for example, Elinor Dashwood's ex-cessively rigid and stoical conception of propriety sometimes does. Yet

From *Those Elegant Decorums: The Concept of Propriety in Jane Austen's Novels*. ©1973 by the State University of New York. State University of New York Press, 1973.

Elizabeth's standards of propriety, at least at the close of the novel, are being presented as identical to the best standards of proper behavior held by her society, as well as identical to the standards of the novel as a whole—and so conformist an ethic might be expected to offend modern readers.

Jane Austen manages to get her readers—even most of her twentieth-century readers—to approve Elizabeth's adherence to a socially acceptable standard of propriety by employing a variety of subtly concealed persuasive techniques. The definition of true propriety which *Pride and Prejudice* offers—to anticipate somewhat—is simply a healthy respect for the conventional rules of social behavior, modified by an understanding that those forms are important, not as ends in themselves, but as means of regulating social intercourse, and that therefore they need not always be followed slavishly.

Jane Austen here seems to be dividing rules of propriety into two classes: those rules that represent the social codification of basic moral principles, and those that are primarily matters of fashion or convenience. This division does not correspond to the division of propriety into minor rules (governing everyday social interaction) and major rules (governing the handling of the most important social and familial relationships, as well as behavior in crucial and dangerous social situations) that is important in *Sense and Sensibility*. All the major rules, in terms of *Sense and Sensibility*'s division, clearly fall within the class of basically moral rules in terms of *Pride and Prejudice*'s division. However, the minor rules, considered in *Sense and Sensibility* as a unit, are divided in *Pride and Prejudice* between the class of basically moral minor rules and the class of minor rules that are merely matters of convenience. . . . An example of a minor rule that is basically moral in character is the rule against breaking a first engagement because one has received a second invitation. An example of a minor rule that is a matter of fashion or convenience only is the rule prohibiting young ladies from taking long country walks by themselves. The implication in *Pride and Prejudice* is that people of true propriety always respect both major and minor rules of propriety which have an important moral element because it would be immoral to do otherwise, but respect rules that are matters of fashion and convenience only where they seem to be reasonably functional and sensible (in practice this turns out to be most of the time). The validity of those rules of propriety which have an important moral element (a class which includes all the major rules as they are defined in *Sense and Sensibility*, as well as many minor rules) is not seriously questioned in this novel.

The first aspect of this definition of propriety—that individuals ought generally to respect the conventional rules of social behavior, especially where those rules have a significant moral element—is a tacit assumption in *Pride and*

Prejudice. Jane Austen does not state this idea overtly, perhaps because she senses that the bald statement of so conformist a norm might alienate some readers and, at any rate, could hardly be found novel or intriguing, but she enforces it vigorously, nonetheless, by using all her charm as a humorous writer to lure her readers into participating in her censure of *all* those characters who fail to respect the conventional forms of decorum. *Pride and Prejudice* contains no character, like Mrs. Jennings or Admiral Croft, whose impropriety of behavior is actually a clue to internal worth—Mrs. Jennings's impertinent curiosity, in fact, indicating, at least in part, her warm and generous interest in other people, Admiral Croft's impulsiveness indicating exuberant good feeling—so that the reader, whether he realizes it or not, is being manipulated into feeling that the forms of propriety are very desirable. Indeed, Jane Austen is very careful, in *Pride and Prejudice*, to give her readers precise characterizations of the manners of most of her important characters very close to their first appearances in the novel, and perhaps one of her reasons for following this rather uncharacteristic procedure is her desire to make absolutely sure that her readers do not begin by making the erroneous assumption that unattractive characters like Miss Bingley can ever have really well-bred manners (and thus we get fairly accurate descriptions of Bingley's manners, Darcy's manners, Miss Bingley and Mrs. Hurst's manners, Sir William Lucas's manners, Elizabeth's manners, Jane's manners, and so forth).

However, Jane Austen is much more explicit in defining the second aspect of her idea of true propriety in this novel: that is, her belief that all the forms of propriety are there for a purpose (be that purpose basically moral or basically a matter of social convenience) and hence are being perverted if they are treated as ends in themselves. The incident of Elizabeth's solitary three-mile walk to Netherfield, which occurs very early in the novel, embodies the views on the purpose of the forms of decorum which the novel as a whole enforces, in a clear and unambiguous way. Jane Bennet, who has been visiting Netherfield, has fallen ill there and Elizabeth "feeling really anxious was determined to go to her, though the carriage was not to be had; and as she was no horsewoman, walking was her only alternative." The situation here is thus set up most plainly. Elizabeth has a very valid reason for wishing to go to Netherfield (we learn later that Jane "longed for such a visit"), and walking is her only means of getting there. Readers are obviously meant to feel that the rules of propriety prohibiting solitary cross-country hikes for young ladies—rules which are concerned with the neatness of the lady's appearance and the possible danger to her consequent upon making a practice of walking long distances alone—ought rationally to be set aside in this unusual situation. In taking a three-mile walk, Elizabeth, as she is well aware, breaks no moral law. And in fact, by their reactions to this crucial and unambiguous decision on a point of decorum, Jane Austen allows several of her characters to reveal what sort of stuff they are made of. "'You will not be fit to be seen when you get there,'" cries Mrs. Bennet, proving once again both that she has no idea of what is really important in social behavior and that she regards her daughter as merchandise on display. "'Every impulse of feeling should be guided by reason . . . exertion should always be in proportion to what is required,'" says Mary Bennet, revealing the fact that she completely fails to understand what is required by Elizabeth's love for Jane. "'We will go as far as Meryton with you,'" say Kitty and Lydia, uninterested in theoretical questions of propriety in the heat of their own headlong pursuit of officers. "'It seems to me to show . . . a most country-town indifference to decorum,'" says Miss Bingley, a social climber who values herself on the elegance and fashion of her own behavior, which, however, is often contemptuous and rude. The good-natured, unpretentious Bingley is able to see that Elizabeth's walk "shows an affection for her sister that is very pleasing." And Mr. Darcy, admiring "the brilliancy which exercize had given [Elizabeth's] complexion," but doubting "the occasion's justifying her coming so far alone" reveals both a basic understanding of what good manners are and a characteristic tendency to place too much stress on preserving the forms of gentility, a tendency that results from pride in his own high social status. Thus, the incident of Elizabeth's walk defines explicitly what might be called the functional aspect of the *Pride and Prejudice* ideal of propriety and smaller incidents of similar import later in the novel—such as the one in which Elizabeth defends the right of younger sisters to come out socially before the elder ones are married—prevent the reader from forgetting the point.

By failing to live up to the novel's ideal of propriety—a respect for the conventions of propriety modified by an understanding that those conventions are not ends in themselves—or by revealing the fact that their concept of proper behavior differs from that suggested by the novel as a whole, the characters in *Pride and Prejudice* reveal their own moral shortcomings. And it is not merely that something vaguely wrong with the manners is a clue to something vaguely wrong with the character, for in fact the flaw in the manners usually turns out to be a very precise counterpart to the moral flaw in question. A significant example of the way this concept works can be seen in the character of Charlotte Lucas. Charlotte is a sensible, well-meaning young woman, and her manners are generally polite and unaffected. In fact, Charlotte is guilty of only one real breach of propriety in the course of the novel, but this breach is very significant, for it provides an unambiguous clue to the moral flaw which will eventually cause Charlotte to marry Mr. Collins and become the sycophantic dependent of Lady Catherine de Bourgh. Charlotte arrives to visit the Bennet family immediately after Elizabeth has refused Mr. Collins's proposal of marriage. As she is sitting with Mrs. Bennet and the girls, Mr. Collins enters, and on perceiving him, Mrs. Bennet says, "'Now I do insist upon it that you, all of you . . . let Mr. Collins and me have a little conversation together.'" Elizabeth, Jane, and even Kitty "passed quietly out of the room" at this request, but Charlotte "detained at first by the civility of Mr. Collins . . . and then by a little curiosity, satisfied herself by walking to the window and pretending not to hear." In fact, Charlotte eavesdrops on the whole conversation and this tiny incident contains the key to Charlotte's character. Elizabeth and Jane, with their delicate sense of personal honor, would consider it beneath them to eavesdrop on any conversation, however interesting. But Charlotte is perfectly willing to satisfy her curiosity (which, of course, reveals her interest in Mr. Collins) in this underhand way, for it is the fault of her character that she lacks firm principle and the sense of personal integrity that make one obey one's conscience when it dictates the sacrifice of personal advantage. Thus, by this minor act of impropriety, Charlotte reveals the traits which will later make it possible for her to violate principle in order to marry, for security, a man she does not love and to court, for advancement, a woman she cannot respect. A woman who marries Mr. Collins, says Elizabeth, "'cannot have a proper way of thinking . . . though it is Charlotte Lucas!'" and it is precisely her improper way of thinking that Charlotte's improper manners would have demonstrated to Elizabeth, had Elizabeth observed those manners more closely.

And as Charlotte's manners reveal her character flaw so precisely, so do the manners of virtually all the other characters in the novel. Sir William Lucas and Mr. Collins are both, in different ways, so enamored of the forms of civility that the purpose of those forms has largely been forgotten. Sir William occupies "himself solely in being civil to all the world," hardly a worthy lifetime occupation. Mr. Collins has fallen deeply in love with two of the commonest forms of politeness — the apology and the thank you — and has completely failed to understand that those forms have definite functions in social intercourse. Thus, he bestows his thanks liberally on people who have absolutely no claim to his gratitude — as when he thanks Lady Catherine "for every fish he won" from her at cards. And, by the same token, he apologizes when he cannot possibly have offended — at cards again "apologizing" to Lady Catherine "if he thought he won too many [fish]." The fact that both these characters are so concerned with empty forms of propriety reveals both their empty heads and their purposeless lives. Another group of characters misunderstand or ignore the forms of politeness in various ways. Mrs. Bennet addresses those who please her "with a degree of civility which made her two daughters ashamed," but is frankly rude to anyone who crosses her, and this inconsistency of manners is just one more example of Mrs. Bennet's characteristic tendency to judge and react to things entirely as they affect her as an individual, completely disregarding any function they may serve in the world as a whole. " 'I do think it is the hardest thing in the world that your estate should be entailed away from your own children; and I am sure if I had been you I should have tried long ago to do something or other about it,' " she tells her husband. Good manners to Mrs. Bennet are just one more way of getting what she wants, and she has failed to teach her daughters Kitty and Lydia, "always unguarded and often uncivil," anything at all about the importance or function of decorous behavior. Lydia's tendency to ignore the rules of propriety without thinking anything much about them is the clue to her more serious decision to ignore the rules of morality in living with a man who has not married her ("she was sure they would be married sometime or other and it did not much signify when"). Lydia ignores both propriety and morality in an unthinking pursuit of personal satisfaction. Miss Bingley and Mrs. Hurst "were in the habit . . . of associating with people of rank. . . . They were of a respectable family . . . a circumstance more deeply impressed on their memories than that their brother's fortune and their own had been acquired by trade." They hope to succeed with the nobility and place a good deal of stress on elegance and fashion in manners, but they reveal their lack of true gentility in their willingness to be rude to social inferiors like Elizabeth. Lady Catherine's dictatorial and condescending manners toward those she considers socially inferior reveal her pride of rank as well as the fact that she is uninterested in judging people by their inherent worth. Mr. Bennet's manners are in a class by themselves, for he is clever enough to be able to pervert the forms of politeness—which he, unlike the characters discussed above, thoroughly understands—into a weapon which he uses against those whom he despises. " 'My dear,' " he says to Mrs. Bennet, masking insult under the forms of courtesy, " 'I have two small favors to request. First, that you will allow me the free use of my understanding on the present occasion; and secondly, of my room. I shall be glad to have the library to myself as soon as may be' "—an offensively polite way of saying shut up and get out. Thus Mr. Bennet makes the forms of politeness serve the purposes of his contempt for others. And in a similar manner Mr. Bennet perverts his considerable talents ("talents which rightly used, might at least have preserved the respectability of his daughters"), using them not to serve any desirable end, but merely to increase his idle amusement at the follies of a family to which he should have taught better behavior.

Many other examples could be given of the way in which manners mirror the moral character in the world of *Pride and Prejudice,* for this is true of nearly every character in the novel. And this is an important difference between *Sense and Sensibility* and *Pride and Prejudice.* In *Sense and Sensibility,* the rules of propriety are ultimately justified by their connection with the concept of duty—and true propriety consists in following them to the letter, even when they oppose personal judgment and feeling. This is a very exacting and theoretical standard of propriety and perhaps that is why Jane Austen does not assume that to fall below this high standard is invariably evidence of real immorality. Thus, Mrs. Jennings's frequent improprieties are signs that she has not always lived in good society and that her friendly interest in others is sometimes carried to an uncomfortable pitch —but not that she is in any sense a bad person. Mrs. Jennings does not have Elinor's sophisticated understanding of the function of a code of propriety in the social system, but she can still be a good woman in her less stoical and intellectual way. Also, since the external manifestation of *Sense and Sensibility*'s code of true propriety consists simply of obeying all the major and minor rules of propriety to the letter, it can easily be followed by those unfeeling, unintelligent people, like Lady Middleton, who have few personal desires or judgments urging them to disobey. But *Pride and Prejudice*'s standard of propriety suggests that the truly proper individual must disobey the rules whenever sound common sense and good morality approve—so that only people possessing these two important attributes *can* live up to the novel's ideal of propriety, even in a purely external sense. That is why improper characters must be either immoral or stupid in *Pride and Prejudice,* but not in *Sense and Sensibility.*

And, as one might expect, this idea of manners as an outward manifestation of inward moral value plays an important role in the main theme of the novel: Elizabeth's proud and prejudiced misjudgment of Darcy and Wickham. In tracing how Elizabeth's misjudgment of Darcy and Wickham's manners contributes to her misjudgment of their characters, we shall see that manners mirror character so closely in *Pride and Prejudice* that the problem of judgment is reduced almost entirely to a problem of evaluating outward social manners. Darcy's relationship with Elizabeth begins in an act which she perceives as an act of rudeness. At the first Meryton ball attended by Bingley's party, Bingley suggests that Darcy, who is not dancing, stand up with Elizabeth. "'Which do you mean?'" asks Darcy, "and turning round, he looked for a moment at Elizabeth, til catching her eye, he withdrew his own and coldly said, 'She is tolerable, but not handsome enough to tempt me; and I am in no humor at present to give consequence to young ladies who are slighted by other men.'"

Elizabeth, needless to say, is not pleased with this comment, which implies that she is both unattractive and unpopular, and she views the remark as a definite piece of rudeness. But the mere fact that her mother shares this view — for Mrs. Bennet later "related with much bitterness of spirit and some exaggeration, the shocking rudeness of Mr. Darcy" to her husband — ought to make us suspicious. And, in fact, when examined more closely, Darcy's remark, though certainly not good-natured or friendly, need not be seen as actually rude. For Darcy, after all, has been rudely insulting to Elizabeth only if he intended her to over-hear his remark, and on this point we have no evidence (except that his with-drawing his eye on catching Elizabeth's may indicate that he didn't want her to notice his observation). Conversations in crowded rooms are frequently over-heard in Jane Austen's novels. Given Jane Austen's passion for verisimilitude of detail, we can probably assume that she would not have used this device repeatedly if she were not convinced that people are often unaware how far their voices can carry through a crowd buzzing with conversation, to the ears of an alert, inter-ested listener. Possibly, Darcy *is* unaware that Elizabeth has been watching him with great interest and is listening sharply enough to catch tones which he assumes are inaudible to her. At this very same Meryton ball, we later learn, Charlotte Lucas, who likes to overhear things, has overheard Mr. Robinson ask Bingley "Whether he did not think there were a great many pretty women in the room, and *which* he thought the prettiest? and his answering immediately to the last question—Oh! the eldest Miss Bennet without a doubt, there cannot be two opinions on that point." Now one might validly consider it rude for Mr. Robinson and Mr. Bingley to discuss Jane Bennet's superior charms in Charlotte's hearing, but Charlotte is not vain of her looks and the Bennet family is pleased that Bingley admires Jane, so no one even thinks to accuse these gentlemen of rudeness. But readers are obviously meant to contrast this incident with the almost simultaneous one in which Elizabeth overhears Mr. Darcy—" '*My* overhearings were more to the purpose than *yours,* Eliza,' " says Charlotte, underlining the similarity—and to conclude that the Bennets are not completely justified in their belief that Darcy has been very rude to Elizabeth, and that they have jumped to that conclusion primarily because the overheard remark was so unflattering in nature. Darcy's remark certainly indicates that his character is seriously flawed. It is ungracious, snobbish, and shows a desire to think poorly of others, but it does not necessarily show (as Elizabeth believes) a willingness to break important, morally oriented rules of propriety, like the rule that one should not wound others by openly displaying contempt for them.

Elizabeth chooses to view Darcy's remark as an act of rudeness, and until the revelation of his true character in the middle of the novel, she continues to inter-pret his least offensive behavior as incivility. And, in fact, Jane Austen is ex-tremely careful to show her readers that after the remark at the ball—which may or may not have been intentionally rude—Darcy's behavior to Elizabeth is not in-variably gracious, but at least invariably polite. When Sir William, whose too civil manners are always embarrassing, distresses Elizabeth by offering her to Mr. Darcy as a dancing partner, Darcy requests the honor of her hand "with grave propriety" which entirely escapes her notice. When Mrs. Hurst and Miss Bingley openly slight Elizabeth at Netherfield, "Mr. Darcy felt their rudeness" and tries to remedy it, though Elizabeth once again ignores him. He addresses Jane on her recovery from a bad cold "with a polite congratulation," and makes "polite inquiries" of Elizabeth at the Netherfield ball. But Elizabeth's opinion of Darcy's manners has been fixed on the basis of his first ambiguous slight, so that when he asks her to dance a reel, she is certain he wishes to despise her taste, and when he watches her playing and singing, is sure he is rudely trying to alarm her. From the first, she tells him later, "your manners impressing me with the fullest belief of . . . your selfish disdain of the feelings of others, were such as to form that groundwork of disapprobation, on which succeeding events have built so immovable a dislike." Elizabeth, noticing only Darcy's ungraciousness, sees his manners as selfish and rude, when Jane Austen is at pains to show her readers that those manners are often awkward and cold, but consistently polite.

But Elizabeth thinks that Darcy's manners are rude and that his rudeness indicates both a lack of respect for others and a lack of moral principle. She believes Wickham's slander of Darcy in part because she believes that Darcy does openly violate the important, morally oriented laws of propriety — and she reasons that one who violates the dictates of this sort of law of propriety is very likely to violate the dictates of pure morality also, even to the point of disregarding a clause in his father's will leaving a living to a man he dislikes. And, as we have seen, this is a perfectly valid way to reason in the world of *Pride and Prejudice* — Elizabeth's reasoning here does precisely apply to her sister Lydia, though it is unfair to Darcy. Elizabeth is wrong about Darcy, not because his manners lie about his character, but because she has misperceived those manners. Darcy is, in fact, quite polite in a formal sense (even if we are unwilling to assume from his decorous behavior afterwards that he did not really intend Elizabeth to overhear his remark at the ball, still this is his only possible act of true impropriety), and what Elizabeth repeatedly identifies as real rudeness is actually something quite different: an ungraciousness of manner resulting mainly from an excessive sense of social and personal superiority. When Darcy, at the end of the novel, tells Elizabeth that "'I was taught what was right, but I was not taught to correct my temper. I was given good principles, but left to follow them in pride and conceit,'" he gives an accurate description of what his manners originally were. Convinced of his own superiority — and, incidentally, also shy — Darcy preferred despising his acquaintances to taking the trouble of getting to know them, but he never lacked respect — as Elizabeth thought — for the sensible and moral conventions of decorum and to be strictly well-mannered was always an important part of his self-image. The narrator, accurately as it turns out, remarks that his manners "though well-bred, were not inviting." Elizabeth's basic mistake in her estimate of Darcy's character was her conclusion that because he hurt her feelings, he was being intentionally rude to her and that therefore his manners were of the ill-bred sort that indicate a basically flawed moral character. Elizabeth's misperception of Darcy's character is thus integrally related to her misperception of his manners.

Just as an affront to her pride produces Elizabeth's prejudiced and distorted view of Darcy's manners, so Wickham's flattering behavior to her at the very opening of her acquaintance with him leads Elizabeth to misjudge radically the nature of his manners and hence of his moral character. When Elizabeth first meets Wickham, she is already fairly well-acquainted with Mr. Darcy and has formed her low opinion of his manners and morals. Wickham's fabricated tale of Darcy's unprincipled behavior toward him therefore confirms an opinion to which Elizabeth is already emotionally committed, and hence she wishes—though she does not quite realize it—to credit Wickham's story. Further, the fact that Wickham tells his intimate story to her, a stranger, and to her alone, flatters Elizabeth. It is naturally more pleasing to Elizabeth to view Wickham's confidences to her as a discerning compliment not only to her attractiveness, but also to her obvious intelligence and discretion—for, after all, she *can* be trusted not to spread rumors—than it is for her to regard these confidences as secrets which it is categorically improper to relate to a stranger under any circumstances. Therefore, Elizabeth, though she is unaware of this fact, has a substantial emotional interest in believing Wickham's story and since believing his story necessarily involves believing in Wickham's character, Elizabeth must persuade herself that Wickham's manners, as a clue to his character, are well-bred and unexceptionable.

Wickham's manners are, in fact, superficially polished and charming. On first seeing him, Elizabeth notes his "gentlemanlike appearance . . . and very pleasing address . . . perfectly correct and unassuming." The narrator does not set the reader straight concerning the true nature of Wickham's manners (as she does with Darcy), but Wickham's behavior quickly reveals to the reader, if not to the already prejudiced Elizabeth, that his manners are not really so gentlemanlike as they at first appear. In his first long conversation with Elizabeth about Darcy's character, Wickham's behavior is improper in the extreme. Such communications about the son of his benefactor should never, of course, be made to an absolute stranger. Wickham is well aware of this and tries to defend himself against possible charges of impropriety and ingratitude by asserting that he would never do the very thing that he is in fact doing. "'Til I can forget [Mr. Darcy's] father, I can never defy or expose him,'" he tells Elizabeth in the midst of his very complete exposé of Darcy's supposed inhumanity to him. Elizabeth herself is prevented by her instinctive sense of personal honor from asking Wickham any questions about Darcy, realizing that "the delicacy of [the subject] prevented farther inquiry," but she fails to reflect that a subject on which it is improper to make inquiries is probably one which should not be discussed at all. Wickham's manners on this occasion mirror his most basic character flaws. For his impropriety actually reveals the lack of respect for the important rules of decorum and the moral principles which stand behind those rules that Elizabeth wrongly thought she perceived in Darcy. And "the inconsistency of his professions with his conduct" reveals Wickham's fundamental hypocrisy. Thus Wickham's basically bad moral character has been obvious in his manners from the beginning, as Elizabeth realizes after reading Darcy's justification of his conduct to Wickham. "She was *now* struck with the impropriety of such communications to a stranger and wondered it had escaped her before." And Elizabeth is later able to realize, too, that the warmth and gentleness that always mark Wickham's manners are sometimes very inappropriate to the situations in which he is involved. Elizabeth is convinced that one ought to judge other people on the basis of individual worth, uninfluenced by any considerations of social status. She originally regards Darcy's invariable hauteur as a sign that he has rejected all Meryton society for purely snobbish reasons and sees Wickham's warmth as a generous response to real merit. But ultimately Elizabeth realizes that just as Darcy's excessive stiffness is mistaken and offensive, so in Wickham's invariable gentleness there is a "sameness to disgust and weary," and when Wickham behaves warmly and affectionately to the family of the girl he has seduced and married only under the inducement of bribery, Elizabeth realizes that dignity and suitability to the occasion are much more important elements in good manners than warm responsiveness.

Wickham's manners on the occasion of his first long talk with Elizabeth are very bad, but afterwards they become even more obviously improper, for he abruptly drops Elizabeth to pay court to a young lady who has suddenly acquired £10,000 and of whom he had not taken the slightest notice prior to that event. Elizabeth's emotional commitment to her belief in Wickham's good character is such, however, that she undertakes to convince herself that her friend's manners are at all times unexceptionable, that he is always "her model of the amiable and pleasing." And in her attempt to convince herself that Wickham's bad manners are really good manners, Elizabeth is forced to distort her own conception of propriety to the point where it becomes invalid. Elizabeth, as we have seen, is originally a sensible advocate for a mild degree of individual discretion on minor questions of decorum. She thinks that minor rules of propriety which are merely matters of fashion or convenience may sometimes be violated, but she does not by any means condone violating rules of propriety that are closely connected with moral principles. She is also a believer in human relationships based on mutual esteem. So when Wickham makes his improper confidences to her, Elizabeth's pleasure in the intimacy they have established makes her justify to herself as reasonable and sensible what is actually an unjustifiable breach of propriety. And when Wickham pays his attentions to the newly rich Miss King,

Elizabeth fails to reflect—as she justly did when Charlotte accepted Mr. Collins—that it is immoral to marry solely for money and truly indecorous to pursue a woman merely because she has suddenly become wealthy. In fact, when her aunt, Mrs. Gardiner, points out the "indelicacy" of Wickham's behavior, Elizabeth replies that "'A man in distressed circumstances has not time for all those elegant decorums which other people may observe.'" We must recall Elizabeth's walk to Netherfield—an occasion on which she showed herself willing to break a minor law of decorum for a very worthy and valid motive—to realize how Elizabeth's concept of good breeding has become coarsened and falsified under the stress of her need to believe in Wickham's good manners and character. Here she classes what is, in fact, a law of decorum with a vital moral element—that a man should not court a rich girl for whom he obviously does not care at all—with the sort of rule of decorum, like the one prohibiting solitary female walking, that is entirely a matter of fashion and convenience. In her desire to justify Wickham, Elizabeth has confused the moral and fashionable aspects of propriety and has moved to an unjustifiably libertarian concept of manners.

When Darcy's explanatory letter finally opens Elizabeth's eyes to Wickham's true character and the need to justify his behavior disappears, Elizabeth understands the mistakes into which she has fallen and is horrified. When her unprincipled sister Lydia remarks without censure that Wickham had never cared about the "nasty, little, freckled" Miss King, "Elizabeth was shocked to think that . . . the coarseness of the *sentiment* was little other than her own breast had formerly harbored and fancied liberal." So Elizabeth reverts to something like her original view of the nature of good manners, and the only change is that she now places a somewhat greater stress on the importance of conventional propriety than before. It is after she realizes the error of her libertarian views that Elizabeth becomes deeply concerned about the impropriety of behavior that has characterized her own family. Previously this impropriety had embarrassed Elizabeth, but she had not regarded it as very important. But now she considers it most seriously and even takes the rather remarkable step (remarkable because, in the world of Jane Austen, even very deficient parents invariably receive scrupulous outward respect) of advising her father that it is his duty to attempt to correct "Lydia's unguarded and imprudent manner." Further, she is now able to realize that, though Darcy's manners have lacked graciousness, the strict propriety which has generally marked them is most valuable as evidence of sound and firm moral values.

And as Elizabeth's manners become more formal, Darcy's manners are also changing. He is shocked by Elizabeth's charge that his manners are not "gentlemanlike" and decides that she is at least partially correct ("'My behavior . . . merited the severest reproof'"). Darcy censures himself for the stiff and haughty manners that reveal his wish "'to think meanly of all the rest of the world,'" on very insufficient evidence. When he encounters Elizabeth at Pemberley, Darcy is determined to show her that his manners now exhibit true consideration for others, as well as merely formal politeness. His behavior at Pemberley to her socially inferior merchant relatives, the Gardiners, as Mrs. Gardiner herself remarks, was "'more than civil, it was really attentive; and there was no necessity for such attention'" according to the ordinary rules of propriety. By his considerate and polite manners toward the Gardiners, Darcy shows both that his worst character flaw—the desire to look down on other people, particularly those of lower status—and his overly formal concept of propriety, have been corrected. Meanwhile, Elizabeth has mended her own tendency to disregard the strict rules of propriety a bit too readily ("'my behavior to *you* was at least always bordering on the uncivil'"). So both she and Darcy move closer to the ideal of propriety enforced by the novel as a whole—principled respect for the rules of decorum, combined with an intelligent realization that merely to obey the rules in their strictest sense does not constitute the whole of good breeding—as they move closer to each other.

It seems paradoxical that *Pride and Prejudice,* probably Jane Austen's most popular novel and certainly the one that gives readers the greatest sense of the individual's right to be different, is the only one of Jane Austen's books, except for *Northanger Abbey,* that assumes a simple, direct relationship between conventional good manners and good moral character. It is precisely because Jane Austen manages to convince her readers, in this novel, that the laws of morality manifest themselves socially in terms of the laws of propriety—an association that is made linguistically again and again in the course of *Pride and Prejudice:* "folly and indecorum," "decency and virtue," and so forth—that we can accept the idea that her most attractive characters choose socially conventional modes of behavior freely, as a means of realizing their best potentialities. Perhaps part of the charm of *Pride and Prejudice* is to be found in the way it subtly convinces readers that what the intelligent individual wants for himself and what society wants him to be are virtually one and the same, that Elizabeth Bennet is free to be Elizabeth in the best sense, and, in addition, to be the ideal mistress of Pemberley.

Affection and the Amiable Man

Stuart M. Tave

The first time Elizabeth Bennet sees Mr. Darcy, before they have ever spoken to each other, he mortifies her. It is the beginning of their action. His character has been decided already, by all the principal people in the room; Bingley has such amiable qualities as must speak for themselves, but—what a contrast between him and his friend!—Darcy is the proudest, most disagreeable man in the world. Before the action ends Elizabeth will have to discover that this is a really amiable man, to whom she must give her affection. She will have to define the differences between the agreeable and the amiable and to define the foundations of affection; and he will have to become worthy of that process of painful definition. It will be a mortifying experience for both of them. Elizabeth has wit and intelligence, a mind that runs with rapid play and liveliness. She finds life more amusing than others do because she is superior in discernment and abilities, so quick in observation and decisive in judgment at the first interview; she will discover a slower and seemingly "less interesting mode" far more interesting, more full of real life.

It will be a long time before she can say of Darcy that he is an "amiable" man, because it is a long time before she knows what the word means. It is a word that can be used lightly, as she has been using it, but not by those who weigh their words. Before Frank Churchill comes to Highbury Emma and Mr. Knightley are arguing about him and the argument, as Mr. Knightley attempts unsuccessfully to give it some precision, turns upon a definition. Emma has called Frank "an amiable young man." Not only is she unacquainted with him but she is, when she uses the phrase, offering a general proposition about a young man of a certain type; to Mr. Knightley it is a weak, indecisive type. There is in

From *Some Words of Jane Austen.* © 1973 by The University of Chicago. The University of Chicago Press, 1973.

some weak people an amiability that is an inactive, docile good temper; it is what Mr. Woodhouse has and Isabella, the daughter who is more like him; it is the kind of thing Captain Wentworth finds in Henrietta Musgrove and, when he knows her faults better, in Louisa. But that is not what Mr. Knightley means by real amiability. Nor is it quite what Emma meant, who had something more agreeable in mind and, without realizing it, something more dangerous. Emma is surprised at the heat of the reaction she has provoked in Mr. Knightley, for several reasons, but she had spoken the word casually, as a conventional epithet of praise. It had pervaded the fiction of the late eighteenth century, densely populated by "amiable," "more than amiable," and "most amiable" heroines and heroes.

Some awareness of this novelistic jargon adds a delight to a reading of Jane Austen's juvenilia, because it adds force to the parodic use of the word. One meets an absurdly endless number of amiable characters, like the landlady of the little alehouse in Evelyn, "who as well as every one else in Evelyn was remarkably amiable"; one meets characters who are, over and over, "the amiable Rebecca" (notwithstanding her forbidding squint, greasy tresses, and swelling back). Part of the joke of the "History of England" is the application of the novelistic adjective to kings, queens, and entire realms, with a scholarly exactness: in the reign of Charles I ("This amiable Monarch") "never were amiable men so scarce. The number of them throughout the whole Kingdom amounting only to *five*." The historian herself may be partial, prejudiced, and ignorant but we must take confidence in the value of the History from her own assurance that she is "my no less amiable self." If we are told, in one of these early pieces, that a character is amiable we know it to be perfect: "perfectly amiable," like the young man who was addicted to no vice (beyond what his age and situation rendered perfectly excusable). It is a happy thing to hear in a young lady's account of her education that "I daily became more amiable, & might perhaps by this time have nearly attained perfection." The progress of the young Catherine Morland, from an unsuccessful romantic heroine to a rather more sensible observer of humanity, can be traced: from her beginning point, when she was surprised that she had reached the age of seventeen "without having seen one amiable youth who could call forth her sensibility"; through her exceeding love for Isabella, as she swallows whole James Morland's estimate of that "thoroughly unaffected and amiable . . . most amiable girl"; to the end point where she can clear General Tilney from her grossly injurious suspicions of villainy and still be able to believe, upon serious consideration, that he is "not perfectly amiable." The charming Augusta Hawkins, before she is ever seen by Highbury, is discovered to have every recommendation of person and mind, to be handsome, elegant, highly accomplished, and, it follows by the formula that denotes not a real person but a fiction, "perfectly amiable." The vapid amiable character, familiar to Jane Austen and no danger to her from her earliest years, remained a staple product of novelists and it was one of the dangers she had to mark out for that beginning author, young Anna Austen. A character in Anna's manuscript is at first interesting to Jane Austen "in spite of her being so amiable," obviously an unusual accomplishment; but Anna could not maintain that pitch, so, in a second letter, her aunt loses interest in that character and finds still another who worries her: "I am afraid [he] will be too much in the common Novel style — a handsome, amiable, unexceptionable Young Man (such as do not much abound in real Life)."

To stupid Mr. Collins, a self-conscious master of complimentary terminology that has not much to do with real life, the word is a valuable all-purpose superlative. Miss De Bourgh, he rapidly informs the Bennets, is "perfectly amiable," though the details of her he has offered bear another tale. His cousin Elizabeth, as he tells her with clocklike solemnity during his proposal, also qualifies for the word, though, as he also assures her, there are many other amiable young women in his own neighborhood; and when he transfers his affections to Charlotte he transfers the word as easily. What is more amusing is that in Elizabeth's difficult brief period, following her rejection of Mr. Collins, Charlotte seems to her to be "very amiable" in accepting his attentions; she is thankful to her friend Charlotte for this obliging kindness. Elizabeth has something to learn about amiability. It is something important enough to consider in multiple illustration because it keeps returning in almost all of Jane Austen's writing. To Mr. Knightley it is a point of reality that helps define the national character.

What Elizabeth has to learn is important, because there is a true amiability, not an insipid fictive perfection that offers itself for immediate admiration but a reality that frequently takes time to disclose itself or to be discovered by an observer who is unable to see it. An intelligent young woman, unlike a romantic heroine, will not meet much perfection in her experience but she may well make mistakes in understanding what is more difficult: the difference between those who are truly "amiable" and those who are only "agreeable." That is "an important distinction," Dr. Gregory warned his daughters, "which many of your sex are not aware of" (*A Father's Legacy to His Daughters,* 1774, and many later editions, into the nineteenth century). Jane Austen makes the distinction in two of her letters, writing about the same young man: first in a passing observation to her sister Cassandra, and then, more than a year later, to Fanny Knight, on a critical occasion, which validates the large significance of the words. Mr. John Plumtre, she tells Cassandra, is someone she likes very much: "He gives me the idea of a very amiable young Man, only too diffident to be so agreeable as he might be." He is lacking in the social manner that would make him complete, but a completeness cannot be expected often, and when there are choices to be made it is always the amiable that is to be chosen. Mr. Plumtre then attaches himself to Fanny Knight and Fanny encourages him until she finds that perhaps she has mistaken her own feelings; Jane Austen, as her aunt, tries to give her the best possible advice, not telling her what to do, but clarifying for her what the alternatives are. There is a strong case to be made for Mr. Plumtre, "above all his character—his uncommonly amiable mind, strict principles, just notions, good habits . . . *All* that really is of the first importance." His manners are not equal to this excellence, but a comparison between him and Fanny's own "agreeable, idle Brothers" will show Fanny that it is Mr. Plumtre who has the sterling worth. He is not perfect, because he has a fault of modesty, and if he were less modest "he would be more agreeable, speak louder & look Impudenter," but it is a fine character of which this is the only defect. The conclusion is not that Fanny should marry him—and we'll come back to Mr. Plumtre—but her aunt's advice will lead her to understand her choices and enable her to decide for the right reasons, not reject a man of uncommonly amiable mind and all that is really of the first importance because she thinks it more important that the man be agreeable.

If agreeable men are likely to be suspect characters in Jane Austen there is good cause. Their agreeableness might be an initial value but it would improve upon acquaintance and reveal the mind, principles, notions, and habits that make the moral character, so that the agreeableness of manner and person would not remain the most notable quality. Mr. Elliot of *Persuasion* is that "exceedingly agreeable man," who makes his impression even before his identity is known, who is, in his regard for Anne, a source of agreeable sensation to her; he is offered as a suitable match. "Where could you expect a more gentlemanlike, agreeable man?" But well before she learns the full story of his life Anne has real doubts because she can never find anything more in him. "Mr. Elliot was too generally agreeable," deliberately pleases even where he is contemptuous: even Mrs. Clay "found him as agreeable as anybody," a note in passing that makes the ending of the novel less surprising and more enjoyable. Henry Crawford is more interesting because he is a man who makes an effort to change himself to something better, from "the most agreeable young man" the Miss Bertrams had ever known to a man deserving of the affection of an amiable woman. There is much byplay at Mansfield Park about the mutual agreeableness of the Crawfords and the young Bertrams and even Sir Thomas is impressed by Henry's "more than common agreeableness," the address and conversation pleasing to everyone. Mrs. Price at Portsmouth "had never seen so agreeable a man in her life." It will take more than this to win Fanny but she sees in his visit to Portsmouth that there are ways in which he really is acting differently. In his account of where he has been and what he has been doing there is more than the "accidental agreeableness" of the parties he has been in; he has done good work in performing a duty, for the first time, among the tenants of his estate, thereby securing "agreeable recollections for his own mind"; that is certainly a better kind of agreeableness than he has ever known. She sees that he is much more gentle, obliging, and attentive to other people's feelings than he had ever been at Mansfield: "she had never seen him so agreeable—so *near* being agreeable." Fanny is using the lower word in her own high sense, because he is now near being amiable, and she is making a fine distinction; but she is right, because the good impulse now moving Henry will not be enough. He lacks the principle to maintain the habit of right action. His moral character cannot rise above the agreeable manner. His story ends when he goes to the house of the family at Twickenham where Maria has grown intimate —a family of lively, "agreeable manners, and probably of morals and discretion to suit," for to that house Henry had constant access at all times. What he threw away when he entered that accessible house was the way of happiness, working for the esteem and tenderness that leads to "one amiable woman's affections."

To recognize the one amiable woman, or man, is the first simple perception in making a marriage. In fact few can do it. The lady for whom Willoughby has jilted Marianne is very rich, Elinor learns, but what Elinor wants to know is what kind of woman she is: "Is she said to be amiable?" That is the question because it will determine what can be said for him and what are his chances of happiness, but it was never a question that touched his mind. Edward Ferrars is a better man because the question did concern him, but he had not been able to answer it: Lucy Steele had been successful with him because she "appeared everything that was amiable and obliging." She was not really so, as Elinor has always known, and the mistake he made could have been ruinous in time. The perception of a real amiability requires time. Mrs. Dashwood is correct in her opinion of Edward but her opinion is without much meaning: "It was enough for her that he appeared to be amiable"; to say that he is unlike Fanny Dashwood is enough: "It implies every thing amiable. I love him already." Elinor's measured answer is the right one: "'I think you will like him,' said Elinor, 'when you know more of him,'" because time and knowledge measure possible degrees and truths of feeling. If, therefore, Edward had married Lucy he would have entered a future of great peril. The man who marries an unamiable woman may be made unhappy, but that is not the worst; if he falls in with her manner he may be happy, but he will become an unworthy man. It happened to John Dashwood, who "had he married a more amiable woman" might have improved, "might even have been made amiable himself," for he was very young when he married and very fond of his wife; but Mrs. John Dashwood was a caricature of himself, more narrow-minded and selfish. It happened to Mr. Elton. Emma recognizes that when she sees him as an old married man, to use his own phrase, deliberately hurting

Harriet while smiles of high glee pass between him and his wife. "This was Mr. Elton! the amiable, obliging, gentle Mr. Elton." He is not quite so hardened as his wife but he is growing very like her. There is a littleness about him that Emma had not discovered.

Emma's discovery is a long time in coming because the ability to recognize an amiable man is dependent on the ability to perceive with a moral clarity of definition. Harriet can look forward to being happily married to Mr. Elton, Emma assures her, because "here is a man whose amiable character gives every assurance of it." With the advantage of her long intimacy with Miss Taylor Emma should be able to recognize a "truly amiable woman"; but if she can then say of Harriet that she has never met with a disposition "more truly amiable" the word can have no real meaning for her. She finds Harriet very amiable because of that early and easy deference to herself. Emma cannot distinguish the amiable from the agreeable, uses the words indiscriminately. She has no doubt she has given Harriet's fancy a proper direction when she makes her aware that Mr. Elton is a "remarkably handsome man, with most agreeable manners"; but that is also the language of the talkative Miss Nash, head teacher at Mrs. Goddard's, telling Harriet that beyond a doubt Mr. Elton has not his equal "for beauty or agreeableness." The question Emma puts to Harriet about Robert Martin is precisely the wrong one: "if you think him the most agreeable man you have ever been in company with, why should you hesitate?" The intention of the question, as she points out, is to put another man into Harriet's mind, and it is successful, unfortunately. But it takes a blunt John Knightley to point out an obvious truth: "I never . . . saw a man more intent on being agreeable than Mr. Elton"; Emma has been willing to overlook the labor and the affectation and the working of every feature because it fits her pleasure to think he is a man of good will. Only after he has astonished her by his proposal does she judge him "not . . . so particularly amiable," because at that point it is a great consolation to think so.

Emma needs the agreeable so that she can continue to be comfortable, think a little too well of herself, create her own world without being disturbed by examining it or herself too closely. It is Mr. Knightley, angry with her for misguiding Harriet, who prompts her better self by making things uncomfortable and being "very disagreeable." It is he who gives her hints that she is being neglectful in not visiting the Bateses, not contributing to their scanty comforts, and some hints have come from her own heart—but none is equal to counteract the persuasion of its all being "very disagreeable." When she does call on them, with Harriet, it is not to bring comfort to them but to get rid of what is now the more tiresome subject of Mr. Elton.

The mistake with the agreeable Mr. Elton also makes her rejoice in the coming of Frank Churchill; she hopes to find him agreeable. It was the hope that she was defending against Mr. Knightley when she elicited his critical definition. She has called Frank amiable, but Mr. Knightley makes the distinction for her: "Your amiable young man," if he has not been following his duty instead of consulting expediency, "is a very weak young man." The young man writes fine flourishing letters but he has never exerted himself to pay the proper attention to his father and especially to Mrs. Weston, upon their marriage, so that he has all the external manner and none of the reality of action: "No, Emma, your amiable young man can be amiable only in French, not in English. He may be very 'aimable,' have very good manners, and be very agreeable; but he can have no English delicacy towards the feelings of other people: nothing really amiable about him." But those smooth, plausible manners will be enough, Emma says, to make him a treasure at Highbury, where "We do not often look upon fine young men, well-bred and agreeable"; we must not be nice and ask for virtue too. Her idea of him is that he can adapt his conversation to the taste of everybody and "has the power as well as the wish of being universally agreeable." If he is anything like this he will be insupportable, Mr. Knightley says. But when Frank arrives Emma's vanity gives him every support. She is directly sure that "he knew how to make himself agreeable," as he certainly does; he talks of Highbury as his *own* country and says he has had the greatest curiosity to visit: that he should "never have been able to indulge so amiable a feeling before" passes suspiciously through Emma's brain, but it passes. She only feels that he is agreeable and the rest must wait. The danger to her of the man who knows how to make himself agreeable but who is not amiable multiplies as the story progresses. He even arrives at the point where he is sick of England, which means that in self-pity he is prepared to run from the obligations he owes to the feelings of others. He is, Mr. Knightley had guessed correctly, a weak young man; on the day at Box Hill Jane Fairfax has come to recognize that fact and recognize that he therefore puts his own happiness at the mercy of chance, and hers too. For Emma the moral dangers are even greater because she is readily susceptible to, desirous of, his agreeableness and blind to the rest. In the climactic two hours at Box Hill, when to amuse her "and be agreeable in her eyes" seems all he cares for, Emma is ignorant of his motives and is not sorry to be flattered. As the pitch of the scene rises, in response to his lead Emma loses self-command and insults Miss Bates, pains her, is herself unfeeling. There is an extraordinary pathos and irony when Miss Bates can only reply, "I must make myself very disagreeable, or she would not have said such a thing to an old friend."

The really amiable man, Mr. Knightley teaches us, is the man who is strong in his action because fine in his emotion, who habitually exerts himself to do his duty because he has a delicacy for the feelings of others. He will be a man capable of love and worthy of love. The happiness of Elizabeth Bennet turns upon her ability to recognize the really amiable man; one way of marking her fortunes and progress is to follow her accuracy in assigning the right adjective to the right man and all that it implies of quality of vision. Darcy, we have said, enters the novel with a character quickly determined by the assembly room at the first ball, when his fine person and fortune draw admiration and then, just as quickly, his manners give a disgust. He is discovered to have "a most forbidding, disagreeable countenance." "He was the proudest, most disagreeable man in the world." The immediate contrast is between him and Bingley, whose "amiable qualities must speak for themselves": Bingley soon makes himself acquainted with all the principal people in the room, is lively and unreserved, dances every dance, talks of giving a dance himself at Netherfield. The evidence on either side is hardly existent and Elizabeth will have to do better than all the principal people. She will have to do so in spite of the man himself, in spite of herself, and of their mutually disagreeable introduction. Bingley tries to interest Darcy in Elizabeth as someone very pretty "and I dare say, very agreeable," but he is not tempted. To her Darcy is then "only the man who made himself agreeable no where, and who had not thought her handsome enough to dance with." When, some weeks later, he does ask her to dance she is surprised into accepting him and she frets. "I dare say you will find him very agreeable," says Charlotte, with a small echo. "Heaven forbid! — *That* would be the greatest misfortune of all! — To find a man agreeable whom one is determined to hate! — Do not wish me such an evil."

Bingley, it does develop, is "truly amiable," as Elizabeth later calls him; but even at the time she says that she doesn't know enough of him, and her opinion is still to undergo changes, because Bingley's is a soft amiability that makes him dependent on chance, susceptible to interference by others with his own happiness and therefore with the feelings of the woman he loves. More importantly, Elizabeth's praise of Bingley is offered to emphasize the contrast between him and Darcy and it is delivered to Wickham for that purpose. In response to Wickham's questioning the very first thing she had said of Darcy was "I think him very disagreeable." For that reason she is ready to accept Wickham's story and to think of Darcy as cruel, malicious, unjust, inhumane. Wickham himself she trusts: he is a young man, she says to herself, "whose very countenance may vouch for your being amiable"; and if she thinks of herself as a better judge of character than Jane, she has done no better than Jane will do the next day: "it was not in her nature to question the veracity of a young man of such amiable appearance as Wickham." Jane's less confident nature at least preserves her from Elizabeth's error of deciding the matter against Darcy. More than that, Jane has a good reason for suspending judgment for it is difficult to believe that an intimate friend like Bingley can be so deceived in Darcy's character. The very thought had just occurred to Elizabeth as she listened to Wickham and declared Bingley's amiability but, like several other true thoughts that had come and gone, it did her no good. She is not in love with Wickham, she tells Mrs. Gardiner, "But he is, beyond all comparison, the most agreeable man I ever saw," and the possibility of affection interests her. For all her superior intelligence Elizabeth is more blind than Jane. When Jane thinks that Bingley has departed from her life she has the steadiness not to repine though he "may live in my memory as the most amiable man of my acquaintance." When Elizabeth parts from Wickham, who may now be marrying Miss King, she is convinced that "he must always be her model of the amiable and pleasing." Only Jane has any evidence of the real character of the man she is talking about and Elizabeth has confused the most agreeable man with the model of the amiable. Jane has been crossed in love by the loss of Bingley, which gives her, says Mr. Bennet, a sort of distinction: "Let Wickham be *your* man." "Thank you, Sir," Elizabeth replies, "but a less agreeable man would satisfy me." He would and he does. What she has still to discover is the identity and amiability of that less agreeable man.

Where Wickham has been able to deceive her by false information he has done what he could. As he was maligning Darcy he was also shaking his head over Miss Darcy, professing pain because he could not call her "amiable" — but she was too like her brother in being very, very proud; some months later, in Derbyshire, Elizabeth is prepared to see a "proud, reserved, disagreeable girl," then finds that Miss Darcy is "amiable and unpretending." But Wickham's ability to mislead her where she has never seen the object of his lies is a small thing. The great humiliation is the discovery that she has believed all he says of Darcy because she has been pleased by his preference and offended by Darcy's neglect, therefore courted prepossession and ignorance and driven reason away. The discovery she makes in the receipt of Darcy's letter is less in the new information he offers than in a self-discovery that allows her to see what has always been before her. What she now begins to comprehend is a reality to which she has blinded herself because the appearance was so much more pleasing. That agreeableness, that false amiability of Wickham, had been a charm: it was a countenance, a voice, a manner; as to his "real character" she had never felt a wish of inquiring. She tries now to find some moral reality in her recollection of him, "some instance of goodness," some trait of integrity or benevolence, virtue; she can see him instantly before her in every charm of air and address, but she can remember no "substantial good" beyond the general approbation of the neighborhood or the regard that his social powers had gained him.

The substantial good evaporates as one seeks it in Wickham; as it does in Willoughby, with his uncommonly attractive person and lively manner, which it was no merit to possess; as it does in Mr. Elliot when Anne finds him sensible and agreeable but is still afraid to answer for his conduct. Anne has her own reasons for prizing a man of more warmth and enthusiasm, but the truth about Mr. Elliot's real character, that he has no feeling for others, is the truth about all the very well-mannered and very agreeable young men who, in Mr. Knightley's distinction, have no delicacy toward the feelings of other people, nothing really amiable about them. They can separate their agreeableness from their feeling, so that the pleasing sensations they offer turn terribly chilling. To miss the distinction, then, to be drawn to the agreeable, is shocking, is both an easy and a dangerous temptation, because it is to fall into that pleasing sensation of the unreality that flatters the self. The agreeable imitation of feeling becomes the instant welcome deception. But the real feeling of the amiable man expressing the principle of a life can be known only by the evidences of an earned experience. It may be hard to find that reality, when its appearance is not readily pleasing, and to acknowledge it, however disagreeable to the self.

It was this reality Elizabeth had denied Darcy, as she rejected him and grew more angry and told him directly, in the last sentence that drove him from the room: his manners impressed her with "the fullest belief of your arrogance, your conceit, and your selfish disdain of the feelings of others." As she begins to make the discovery about her blindness she remembers that she has often heard Darcy speak "so affectionately of his sister as to prove him capable of *some* amiable feeling." It is a minimal fact but it has meaning as it follows a new realization of his character—that however proud and repulsive his manners, her acquaintance has given her an intimacy with Darcy's ways and she has never seen anything that betrayed him to be unprincipled or unjust, anything that spoke of irreligious or immoral habits. It has meaning as it precedes her new realization that had his actions been what Wickham represented them, there could be no friendship between anyone capable of those actions and "such an amiable man as Mr. Bingley." She realizes now, when she receives his letter, that she has no evidence to bring against him; as she learns more of the history of his life, when she visits his home, she learns more positively what his behavior has been as child and man. Mrs. Reynolds can testify to his goodness of disposition and to his goodness of action as landlord to tenant and as master to servant. It is a new light on his character. "In what an amiable light does this place him!" Elizabeth thinks, ". . . so amiable a light." But above all she then knows by his conduct to her, who has given him such cause to be an enemy, his capacity for love. She questions him at the end of the story, wanting him to account for having ever fallen in love with her, when her behavior to him had been at least always bordering on the uncivil and when she never spoke to him without rather wishing to give him pain: "Had you not been really amiable you would have hated me for it." He knew no "actual good" of her, she adds; but in fact he did, certainly in her "affectionate behavior" to Jane in need. They are both of them people who are capable of actual good, of affection, really amiable, worthy of love. She knows what he has done for her and her family. By the time Darcy has made his second proposal Elizabeth has learned enough of him and his family to be able to answer her father's doubts of that proud, unpleasant man: "'I do, I do like him,' she replied, with tears in her eyes. 'I love him. Indeed he has no improper pride. He is perfectly amiable.'" It is astonishing praise, and a daring phrase for Elizabeth to use. It is a sign of the pressure of feeling upon her, because her earlier misjudgments and immoderate expressions have forced her into this awkwardness, that she should be so extravagant as to use a kind of novelistic jargon; and it is a sign of Darcy's real excellence that he does not sink under the weight of it. He really is amiable.

The accomplishment of amiability is unusual; it is earned by moral and intelligent effort and it cannot be distributed sentimentally as a reward. The narrator wishes it could be said that Mrs. Bennet's accomplishment of her earnest desire in marrying off her daughters produced so happy an effect as to make her "a sensible, amiable, well-informed woman"; but that could not be, and perhaps it was lucky for her husband, who might not have relished domestic felicity in so unusual a form.

The form in which domestic felicity comes to Elizabeth and Darcy is unusual and it is there not by luck. It comes, first, because both are amiable and that is a necessary foundation, but it comes because on that is built something more. Above all, as Elizabeth knows, there must be love, or to use the word Jane Austen prefers in such contexts, there must be "affection." It is the quieter, more general word, for an emotion of slower growth and more lasting therefor; but it is, in this context, a strong word for a deep emotion. It is the word Emma uses at the moment of her insight into her own heart when she is ashamed of every sensation but one, "her affection for Mr. Knightley"; it is the word Anne Elliot uses to describe her feelings for Captain Wentworth, when he is once again desirous of her affection: "her affection would be his for ever." It is, in general, Jane Austen's chiefest instance of how without the appropriate emotion there is no moral action; specifically it is the love that every marriage must have and without which no married life can stand. Elizabeth Bennet's closest friend calls it into serious question, both in talk and in action, with grave result both for herself and for Elizabeth.

To Charlotte affection is of no importance, except as an appearance that may be useful for getting a husband. She has advice for Jane Bennet, who is very much on the way to being in love but whose composure and cheerfulness do not disclose her real strength of feeling; her advice has nothing to do with the needs of that reality and of the particular characters of Jane and Bingley, for Charlotte's concern is the general method of exploiting the opportunity to fix a man by helping him on with a show of affection. "In nine cases out of ten, a woman had better shew *more* affection than she feels." The love may or may not follow the marriage, but if it does it is a casual supplementary decision that does not require any thought or feeling. "When she is secure of him, there will be leisure for falling in love as much as she chuses." In a word, affection has no real existence for Charlotte. The minor practicality of her advice is that she is right about Bingley's need for encouragement, but she would apply that to any man because the larger need of understanding one's own thoughts and feelings and a mutual understanding of character is what she denies in marriage. The time needed for a developed love is meaningless. To marry tomorrow, to marry after studying character for a twelvemonth, is all the same. "Happiness in marriage is entirely a matter of chance." Knowledge does not advance felicity and it is better to know as little as possible of the defects of the person with whom you are to pass your life. Elizabeth refuses to take her seriously, finds the opinion laughable because it is not sound, because Charlotte knows it is not sound and because Charlotte would never act in that way herself. But Charlotte acts precisely in that way.

There can be no question of any "affection" for or from Mr. Collins, a man to whom the word is known, and known only, as a word which it is customary to employ during a proposal. We have heard him declare himself to Elizabeth shortly before he is secured by Charlotte. "And now nothing remains for me but to assure you in the most animated language of the violence of my affection," where the words and the meaning of the sentence are so marvellously contradictory. Charlotte marries him. "I am not romantic you know," she tells Elizabeth. "I never was." She asks only a comfortable home and considering what she will get with Collins she is convinced that her chance of happiness with him is as fair as most people can boast of on entering the marriage state. Elizabeth's astonishment is so great that it overcomes the bounds of decorum and she cannot help crying out, "Engaged to Mr. Collins! my dear Charlotte, — impossible!" She could not have supposed it possible that when Charlotte's opinions on matrimony were called into action she could have sacrificed every better feeling to worldly advantage. It is, to Elizabeth, a humiliating picture.

One must not be misled by Charlotte's quiet declaration that she is not romantic to think that she is acting in a sensible way in a most difficult situation. What Charlotte does is wrong. But then what ought Charlotte do rather than marry Mr. Collins? She is without much money, she is not handsome, she is no longer young, and to be an old maid without money or position will be an unfortunate life. Miss Bates of *Emma* is an instance and Mr. Knightley lectures Emma on the special consideration Miss Bates's misfortune demands. Miss Bates is in worse condition than Charlotte would be because she has no abilities that can give her respect; Charlotte is intelligent. But that intelligence increases the magnitude of Charlotte's defection, because it makes her match with Mr. Collins the more unequal. He is stupid. He is neither sensible nor agreeable; his society is irksome; and his attachment to her must be imaginary. "But still he would be her husband." And that and his establishment are his total charm. Charlotte is interested in neither the man nor the relationship, only the marriage; and it is not the narrator's but Charlotte's reflection on marriage that "it was the only honourable provision for well-educated young women of small fortune, and however uncertain of giving happiness, must be their pleasantest preservative from want."

There is more than enough evidence, elsewhere in Jane Austen and in this novel, to make clear how mistaken Charlotte is in a decision to marry without affection. The problem of that type of decision returns several times, in minor works and in major, and even in the letters, and the answer is always the same. It is in the first conversation Emma Watson has with her oldest sister. Elizabeth Watson tells bitter tales of their sister, Penelope, who has acted with rivalry and treachery to Elizabeth in the pursuit of a husband, for there is nothing Penelope would not do to get married; at present she is in pursuit of a rich old doctor attacked by asthma. Emma Watson's reaction is sorrow and fear and more than that: to be so bent on marriage, to pursue a man merely for the sake of a situation is shocking to her and she cannot understand it. "Poverty is a great Evil, but to a woman of Education & feeling it ought not, it cannot be the greatest. — I would rather be a Teacher at a school (and I can think of nothing worse) than marry a Man I did not like." Emma Watson is surprised because she is inexperienced, but there is no question that her principles are quite right and that if Elizabeth Watson thinks her too refined it is because Elizabeth herself is, though good-hearted, coarse. Elizabeth's reply, "I think I could like any good humoured Man with a comfortable Income," is one of many signs of her deficiencies. In *Mansfield Park* the great temptation of Fanny Price is to accept the proposal of Henry Crawford, for which every pressure is brought to bear upon her and by those she loves most. But she knows she is doing right in refusing him and she hopes that her uncle's displeasure with her will abate when he considers the matter with more impartiality and comes to feel, as a good man must feel, "how wretched, and how unpardonable, how hopeless and how wicked it was, to marry without affection." We never have any doubt that she is right in this refusal and indeed the whole novel turns on it. It is wicked to marry without affection.

One of Jane Austen's more interesting letters is the advice she wrote to Fanny Knight in 1814 (just after the publication of *Pride and Prejudice* in 1813 and of *Mansfield Park* in 1814), that same letter about the amiable Mr. Plumtre. In it she replies to her niece's anxiety over a grievous mistake, because Fanny has encouraged the young man to such a point as to make him feel almost secure of her — and now her feelings have changed. It was a common mistake, her aunt comforts her, one that thousands of women fall into: he was the first young man who attached himself to her and that was a powerful charm. Furthermore, unlike most who have done the same, Fanny Knight has little to regret, because the young man is nothing to be ashamed of. Jane Austen then goes on to point out all his excellences—his mind, his principles, and all qualities which, as she says, are really of the first importance; the more she writes about him the warmer her feelings grow and the more strongly she feels the sterling worth of such a young man and the desirableness of Fanny's growing in love with him again. She takes up certain objections that Fanny has to him and tries to show her that they are false, that what her niece thinks are faults in him are really unimportant or even advantages. At that point, after such a lengthy, thoughtful, and feeling argument on behalf of the young man, Jane Austen puts into the other side of the balance the one thing that outweighs everything else:

> —And now, my dear Fanny, having written so much on one side of the question, I shall turn round & entreat you not to commit yourself farther, & not to think of accepting him unless you really do like him. Anything is to be preferred or endured rather than marrying without Affection; and if his deficiencies of Manner &c &c strike you more than all his good qualities, if you continue to think strongly of them, give him up at once.

To return, then, from Jane Austen's "my dear Fanny" to Elizabeth Bennet's "my dear Charlotte" and Jane Bennet's "my dear Lizzy" (as they are all addressed in moments of similar crisis): when Elizabeth receives her second proposal from Darcy and accepts him, she seems to the intelligent members of her family, to her father and Jane, to be in a situation similar to Charlotte's when Charlotte accepted Mr. Collins. The similarity is emphasized by a verbal identity. Elizabeth's astonishment had been so great when Charlotte informed her of the engagement to Collins that she could not help crying out, "Engaged to Mr. Collins! . . . impossible!" When Elizabeth is engaged and opens her heart to Jane, the reaction is, untypically for Jane but understandably so, absolute incredulity: "engaged to Mr. Darcy! . . . impossible." Jane's disbelief, unlike Elizabeth's reaction to Charlotte's match, is not that she thinks Darcy without a single quality to make him a desirable husband; on the contrary, nothing could give Bingley or Jane more delight than such a marriage. But she thought it impossible because of Elizabeth's dislike, and even now she cannot approve, however great and desirable it seems, if Elizabeth does not really love him quite well enough. The appeal is direct and deep, and very like Jane Austen's words to Fanny Knight: "Oh, Lizzy! do any thing rather than marry without affection. Are you quite sure that you feel what you ought to do?" So the answer to the question of what Charlotte Lucas ought to do rather than marry Mr. Collins is—"any thing." To be an impoverished old maid is a misfortune, but to marry Mr. Collins is immoral.

Nor is it true that because she has not made the romantic choice, Charlotte has made the practical choice for the comfortable home. The antithesis is false. She had said, in general, that happiness is entirely a matter of chance and she says, in particular, that considering what Collins is, in character, connections, and situation, her chance of happiness with him is as fair as most people can boast on entering the marriage state. But her chances are not even uncertain. That point emerges most convincingly because Charlotte makes the very best of her marriage state and manages it admirably. Elizabeth thinks that it will be impossible for her friend to be tolerably happy but in her visit to Kent she sees how well Charlotte can do. Charlotte maintains her comfortable home and her married life by excluding her husband from it as much as she possibly can. She chooses for her own common use an inferior room with a less lively view because he is less likely to appear in it; Elizabeth gives her credit for the arrangement. She encourages her husband as much as possible in his gardening, to keep him out of the house. When he says something of which she might reasonably be ashamed, which certainly is not seldom, she sometimes blushes faintly, but in general she wisely does not hear. The necessary wisdom for living with Mr. Collins, which Charlotte accepts, is to give up a piece of herself, suppress her shame, lose her ears, see less, diminish her life. As Elizabeth leaves her, at the end of the visit, Charlotte does not ask for compassion, but her prospect is a melancholy one. Her home, housekeeping, her parish and poultry have not yet lost their charms. Not yet. Neither is it a comforting later little note to hear that Mr. Collins's dear Charlotte is expecting a young olive branch. She no doubt will do the best she can, but the children of mismatches without respect or affection do not begin life with advantage.

With her eyes open Charlotte has miscalculated, because there are no fair chances of happiness in an inequality that makes affection impossible. Elizabeth's father can advise his child of this. Like Jane, Mr. Bennet may be mistaken in his facts but not in his principle when he warns Elizabeth to think better before having Mr. Darcy. He knows she cannot be happy or respectable unless she esteems her husband, that an unequal marriage would put her in danger, perhaps discredit and misery. "My child, let me not have the grief of seeing *you* unable to respect your partner in life." He and his daughter know the living experience that speaks in these words. Captivated by youth and beauty and the appearance of good humor they generally give, he had married a woman whose weak understanding and illiberal mind "had very early in their marriage put an end to all real affection for her." The results have been before the reader since the first chapter and before Elizabeth, with less amusement and more pain, all her life. She has felt strongly the disadvantages that must attend the children of so unsuitable a marriage, and Lydia's disaster has confirmed her judgment.

Lydia's affair is, for one thing, what can happen to the child of a marriage without affection. It is, for another, itself an instance of a marriage where neither person is capable of affection. "Her affections had been continually fluctuating" and it required only encouragement for her to attach herself to him in particular. His fluctuations have been apparent to Elizabeth from personal experience; his affection for Lydia, just as Elizabeth had expected, is not equal to hers for him and it is only in fulfillment of the obvious that we hear at the end how "His affection for her soon sunk into indifference." His last private conversation with Elizabeth, in which she makes embarrassingly clear that she knows all about him, ends as he kisses her hand "with affectionate gallantry, though he hardly knew how to look": a very pretty touch that leaves his affection exposed for what it is in a shallow and losing gesture. But, furthermore, the affection of Lydia's Wickham was once something that interested Elizabeth for herself, so that her own understanding of the meaning of affection has not always been what it is at last; it has taken time. If Charlotte Lucas thinks time is unimportant because affection is unimportant, Elizabeth has flirted with another mode in which time is unimportant because affection is so quickly seen. Lydia's affair helps her sister to better understanding.

The validity of the marriage between Darcy and Elizabeth is established by the time in which their affection grows, and by the capacity of the affection to withstand and to be strengthened by the proofs of time and crisis. Elizabeth is certain that the immediate effect of Lydia's disgrace will be that her own power with Darcy must sink, that everything must sink under such a proof of family weakness; it makes her understand her own wishes, and never has she so honestly felt how much she could have loved him as now when all love is vain. The whole of their acquaintance, as she can now review it, has been full of contradictions and varieties and she sighs at the perverseness of her own feelings, which have so changed. In the mode of romance Elizabeth's change is unreasonable or unnatural in comparison with the regard that arises on a first interview and even before two words have been exchanged; but she had given "somewhat of a trial" to this "method" with Wickham and its ill-success might perhaps authorize her to try the other "less interesting mode of attachment." The ironic language sounds like the language of experimental method, and it is that, in the sense of tested experience of common life as opposed to romantic prejudice, but the reality here is the reality of tired emotions. "If gratitude and esteem are good foundations of affection" — and the hypothesis has been tried by Elizabeth's mind and emotions — then the change of sentiment will be "neither improbable nor faulty."

Henry Tilney had come to be sincerely attached to Catherine Morland, he felt and delighted in all the excellences of her character and "truly loved" her society, but, as we know, "his affection originated in nothing better than gratitude."

That may be a new circumstance in romance, but not in common life. "Gratitude" here is the response to the feeling of another, the natural obligation in return for having been thought worthy of being loved. It was this that led Fanny Knight into her mistake with her young man, whose powerful charm was that he was the first young man to attach himself to her. John Gregory, giving fatherly advice to his daughters, warns them that what is commonly called love among girls is rather gratitude and partiality to the man who prefers them to the rest of the sex, so that such a man they often marry with little personal esteem or affection. But the difference between Fanny Knight or Dr. Gregory's daughters and what happens to Elizabeth Bennet is the difference between the young miss and the woman who knows the meaning of affection. In the one the gratitude is the first pleasing stir of a self-love that confuses its object, in the other it is the feeling that initiates a self-discovery. The feeling develops if, as with Darcy, there is a continuing revelation of a character whose actions build more powerful causes of gratitude and if, as with Elizabeth, there is a continuing increase of a character who can perceive and respond to that revelation. Elizabeth's gratitude develops in a heightened vision of him, and in a properly chastened revision of her self-love. That irony, the coolness and detachment of her language, as she recollects how she has arrived at her present feelings by the less interesting mode of attachment, is directed not at her feelings but at herself. She sees in her affection the complicated history of herself. The slow preparation of the foundations creates for an affection its depth of interest and is the guarantee of its reality of meaning in a life. Four months earlier at his declaration of how ardently he admired and loved her she had not been willing to grant Darcy even the conventional gratitude: "In such cases as this, it is, I believe, the established mode to express a sense of obligation for the sentiments avowed, however unequally they may be returned. It is natural that obligation should be felt, and if I could *feel* gratitude, I would now thank you. But I cannot—I have never desired your good opinion." Now she knows by extended experience what his good opinion is worth and what the value of his affection is. Having seen him at Pemberley in a new light, an amiable light, there was then above all, above the respect and esteem, another motive within her, the gratitude she felt for his love of her. It was gratitude not merely for his having loved her, but for loving her still well enough to forgive the petulance and acrimony of her manner in rejecting him and forgive all her unjust accusations. A man who had reason to be her enemy has been eager to preserve her acquaintance, solicit the good opinion of her friends, make her known to his sister. Such a change in such a man excites gratitude, for this is a man who knows something of love, of ardent love.

Furthermore, Darcy's response to the event which she fears has put an end to their acquaintance then becomes the severest test of his affection. He arranges for the marriage of Wickham and her sister and he does it because of "his affection for her." At first she rebukes her vanity for putting so much dependence on the force of that affection, but she has underestimated it. It has remained unshaken, unchanged; when, at last, he can tell her of his feelings, they prove how important she has been to him, and they make "his affection every moment more valuable." That is what enables her to answer her father's doubts of Darcy with "absolute certainty that his affection was not the work of a day, but had stood the test of many months suspense." She is "in the certain possession of his warmest affection."

Love and Pedagogy: Austen's Beatrice and Benedick

Juliet McMaster

"Your lessons found the weakest part," Vanessa complained to her tutor Cadenus, "Aim'd at the head, and reach'd the heart." Swift and Vanessa weren't the first couple, nor yet the last, to discover that the master-pupil relationship can be a highly aphrodisiac one. From Heloise and Abelard to Eliza Doolittle and Henry Higgins, history and literature produce recurrent examples of relations that evolve from the academic to the erotic. And Jane Austen's novels afford in themselves a range of possibilities in the operations of teaching and learning as an emotional bond. As Lionel Trilling points out, Jane Austen "was committed to the ideal of 'intelligent love,' according to which the deepest and truest relationship that can exist between human beings is pedagogic. This relationship consists in the giving and receiving of knowledge about right conduct, in the formation of one person's character by another, the acceptance of another's guidance in one's own growth."

Jane Austen, in exploring this subject so thoroughly, perhaps sets a standard for the nineteenth-century novel, which continued, partly because of its strongly didactic intention, to present love stories in which the heroine falls in love with a man who is her tutor, or her mentor, or her superior in age, experience, or authority. No doubt there is an Oedipal element in the relationship: the daughter is sexually attracted to the embodiment of her father's loving rule. But society generally condones and even encourages this attitude, where it usually looks with disapproval or disgust on the young man who marries the older woman, however wise she may be.

Charlotte Brontë, in spite of her scorn of Jane Austen for knowing nothing of the Passions, nonetheless fastened on the same central relationship for her most

From *Jane Austen on Love.* © 1978 by Juliet McMaster. The University of Victoria, 1978.

passionate attachments. Mr. Rochester is "the master," and Jane, equal soul though she is, looks up to him from the stance of servant, daughter, pupil: "I love Thornfield," she acknowledges; "I love it, because I have lived in it a full and delightful life. . . . I have talked, face to face, with what I reverence; with what I delight in, — with an original, a vigorous, an expanded mind. I have known you, Mr. Rochester" (*Jane Eyre,* chap. 23). Lucy Snowe's relation to Monsieur Paul is literally pedagogic, since he becomes her tutor: "His mind was indeed my library, and whenever it was opened to me, I entered bliss" (*Villette,* chap. 33). Charlotte Brontë, pupil of Monsieur Héger, knew what it was like to be in love with the master, and in her novels she charges the pedagogic relationships with a passion which, though she apparently did not notice it in Jane Austen's novels, she might well have found there in a refined but still intense form.

George Eliot too examined how "potent in us is the infused action of another soul, before which we bow in complete love" (*Daniel Deronda,* chap. 65); but her treatment of the pedagogic relationship differs from Charlotte Brontë's in that it introduces an element of grim irony. Perhaps she remembered with some qualms of embarrassment her adolescent susceptibility to handsome language teachers and elderly pedants, and sought to exorcise the memories. Maggie Tulliver begs Philip Wakem, "Teach me everything — wouldn't you? Greek and everything?" (*The Mill on the Floss,* bk. 2, chap. 6), and he does undertake to develop her and direct her reading, falling deeply in love with her in the process, but her love for him is a thin cerebral quantity that cannot match the force of her strong sexual attraction to Stephen Guest. Dorothea Brooke looks joyfully forward to a marriage in which "she would be allowed to live continually in the light of a mind that she could reverence," but finds that Mr. Casaubon's mind is only a series of dark "vaults where he walked taper in hand" (*Middlemarch,* bk. 1, chaps. 5, 10). And Gwendolen Harleth, eager to receive Deronda's instruction and render herself in return, discovers that though he is ready enough with instruction, he doesn't want *her.*

Henry James goes further still in exploring the sinister implications in the pedagogic relationship. That it fascinated him is testified by his first novel, *Watch and Ward,* which is about a man who brings up his ward, educates her, and marries her at last. But he leads us through a series of disturbing speculations about the right of one mind to govern another, in presenting Maisie, who is used for dubious purposes in the sexual relations of her parents and parent surrogates; Miles and Flora, who apparently either pervert or are perverted by their governess; and Isabel Archer, who negates herself by trying to conform to the aesthetic standards of the manipulators who surround her. The culmination is the horrible premise of the narrator of *The Sacred Fount,* that what one gives — of youth, of wisdom, of joy—is by definition no longer one's own: that the donor becomes, in the process of giving, correspondingly depleted. You can't eat your cake and have it too. When he hears of how much grace and intelligence a certain lady has imparted to a man, he asks incredulously, "She keeps her wit then, . . . in spite of all she pumps into others?" (chap. 1). And he gradually persuades his interlocutor,

> "Whoever she is, she gives all she has. She keeps nothing back—
> nothing for herself."
> "I see—because *he* takes everything. He just cleans her out."
>   (chap. 3)

Similar metaphors are multiplied, until the one who gives is seen as a "victim," the one who receives as "the author of the sacrifice," and we are presented with a complete theory of human relations as a system of parasitism, of society as composed of vampires and victims. The narrator of *The Sacred Fount* may be a crazy hypothesizer, but James gives his theory a certain authority when he returns to the giving and taking relationship again in *The Ambassadors,* where it is hard to resist the conclusion that Chad Newsome has grown fat and sleek while Madame de Vionnet has dwindled to a diaphanous wraith.

Such a progression suggests why Lionel Trilling notes that "the idea of a love based in pedagogy may seem quaint to some modern readers and repellent to others." But he goes on—"unquestionably it plays a decisive part in the power and charm of Jane Austen's art." What to James is suspect and potentially horrible, for Jane Austen is a source of power and charm. For her the pedagogic relationship is not parasitic but symbiotic, a relationship that is mutual and joyful: it blesseth him that gives, and him that takes. The happy resolutions of her novels celebrate the achieved integration of head and heart that is represented by the pupil and teacher coming to loving accord. Novelists of more tragic vision are unable to visualise so complete a reconcilement. A recurring pattern in the novels of the Brontës, George Eliot, Hardy, Lawrence, and others shows a split between the intellectual and the passionate, the Apollonian and the Dionysian, the spiritual and the physical; and the task of the central character is to choose *between* alternatives—between Edgar Linton and Heathcliff, St. John Rivers and Mr. Rochester, Philip Wakem and Stephen Guest, Angel Clare and Alec D'Urberville, Hermione Roddice, and Ursula Brangwen. The final choice may be too difficult, and Cathy, Maggie, and Tess are destroyed in the process of making it; but even where the choice is made and a fortunate resolution achieved, some loss is implied in the rejected alternative.

The alternative men for the Austen heroine—Wickham, Crawford, Churchill, et al.—are far from presenting the same agonising choice of alternatives. Her feelings for them — if aroused at all, which is doubtful — are transitory and swiftly recognized as a delusion. She generally recognizes joyfully that "We needs must love the highest when we see it,/ Not Lancelot, nor another" — and without having to go through the extent of Guinevere's pain and error in the process. The union of Fanny Price with Edmund, say, is entire and satisfying — because Edmund has not only "formed her mind" but also "gained her affections," and at the same time.

Richard Simpson, in his fine early study of Jane Austen, pointed out her commitment to "the Platonic idea that the giving and receiving of knowledge . . . is the truest and strongest foundation of love." But he goes on to suggest that this love between her heroes and heroines doesn't amount to much: "Friendship, to judge from her novels, was enough for her; she did not want to exaggerate it into passionate love." Strongly as he is convinced of her merits, he seems to agree with Charlotte Brontë that the stormy sisterhood of the passions have no place in her work, and that she opts for esteem rather than passion as the basis of a successful marriage. But Jane Austen will not accept that division — for her the full and mutual engagement of head and heart is what *is* passionate; and any substitute, like Marianne's love for Willoughby, is not only founded on a delusion, but a delusion in itself.

The pattern, however, is of course far more varied than this simplification suggests. Ian Watt comments, "As has often been observed, [Jane Austen's] young heroines finally marry older men — comprehensive epitomes of the Augustan norms such as Mr. Darcy and Mr. Knightley. Her novels in fact dramatise the process whereby feminine and adolescent values are painfully educated in the norms of the mature, rational and educated male world." I don't think one needs to be a woman to recognize that as a dangerous generalization. Elizabeth teaches Darcy as much as he teaches her; Anne and Fanny, in the main course of the novels' action, remain morally static while Wentworth and Edmund get the painful education; and Marianne, though she certainly has plenty to learn, learns from her sister. That leaves Catherine and Emma, who do get educated in the norms of their men; but even they have a certain power whereby their Pygmalions find that Galatea has turned the tables on them. . . .

To move from *Northanger Abbey* to *Pride and Prejudice* is like turning from *The Taming of the Shrew* to *Much Ado*. Henry Tilney and Petruchio have it all, or nearly all, their own way, and have comparatively little to learn from their two Catherines; but between Elizabeth and Darcy, as between Beatrice and Benedick, matters are more evenly balanced. They are both student-teachers; not that either deliberately sets out to instruct or to learn from the other — but they do very resoundingly teach each other a lesson. And, again as with Beatrice and Benedick, the state that exists between them is war: "They never meet but there's a skirmish of wit between them" (*Much Ado About Nothing,* act 1).

The similarity between these two gayest of their authors' works sometimes tempts me to speculate whether Jane Austen was consciously following Shakespeare's play. Beatrice, "born in a merry hour" (bk. 2, chap. 1) is surely kin to Elizabeth, who "dearly love[s] a laugh," and her comment, "I was born to speak all mirth and no matter" (bk. 2, chap. 1), seems echoed in Jane Austen's playful assertion that her novel was "rather too light, and bright, and sparkling; . . . it wants to be stretched out here and there with a long chapter of sense, if it could be had."

The analogy is pertinent not only for suggesting the exuberant quality of both works, but for illuminating the sexual piquancy of the love-war relation, that gives such delightful force and suggestiveness to works like *The Rape of the Lock, Pamela, Jane Eyre,* and the wife of Bath's prologue and tale. I find it hard to credit that anyone who has read *Pride and Prejudice* could subscribe to the view of Miss Austen as an old maid who wrote sexless novels — this novel to my ear fairly rings with the jubilant fertility of spring. Elizabeth's physical vitality, expressing itself in her running, her "jumping over stiles and springing over puddles," and so on, is a sexual vitality too; and Darcy's strongly sexual response to her, as he gradually and unwillingly succumbs to her "fine eyes," is quite sufficiently dramatized. We see in Elizabeth as in Beatrice the subsumed attraction that is behind their antagonism — although they always fight with their men, they are always thinking of them. Beatrice, separated as she thinks from Benedick in the masked dance, says almost wistfully, "I would he had boarded me"; and Elizabeth can't see Miss de Bourgh without reflecting, "She looks sickly and cross. — Yes, she will do for him very well" — the "him" in her consciousness being Darcy. But relations between her and Darcy proceed stormily: she refuses to dance with him, and he is the more attracted. When she does dance with him, she quarrels with him about Wickham. They spar in the dance, skirmish at the piano, fence in conversation. Beatrice's sallies on "Signior Mountanto" are echoed in Elizabeth's witticisms at Darcy's expense: "I am perfectly convinced . . . that Mr. Darcy has no defect. He owns it himself without disguise." Such is their "merry war" — very provocative, very delightful.

But the battles are not love play only — they have their serious issues, in which, without usually intending it, the antagonists set up their standards for the other to conform to or reject. Elizabeth is initially closest to being the pedagogue. Bingley recognizes her as "a studier of character"; and in admitting, "Follies and nonsense, whims and inconsistencies *do* divert me, I own, and I laugh at them whenever I can," she achieves the status of a kind of licensed satirist during her brief stay at Netherfield. She makes full use of that licence in her critical analyses of character. In a playful context, she is a teacher catechising a potential student in order to place him:

> "Follies and nonsense, . . . I suppose, are precisely what you are without."
>
> "Perhaps that is not possible for anyone [replies Darcy]. But it has been the study of my life to avoid those weaknesses which often expose a strong understanding to ridicule."
>
> "Such as vanity and pride."
>
> "Yes, vanity is a weakness indeed. But pride—where there is a real superiority of mind, pride will be always under good regulation."
>
> Elizabeth turned away to hide a smile.
>
> "Your examination of Mr. Darcy is over, I presume," said Miss Bingley;—"and pray what is the result?"

"The study of my life," "real superiority of mind," "good regulation," "examination"—this is classroom terminology. And though Darcy goes through this play catechism with the smiling detachment of an adult who has already done with exams, he is to recall and eventually be changed by Elizabeth's standards as implied in these dialogues.

There are three main subjects on which Elizabeth "examines" him in the course of the novel, and in which he acquits himself with varying degrees of credit, at various attempts.

The first issue is his right of influence over Bingley, canvassed at length, in a Netherfield discussion complete with a hypothetical case, as in an exam question. Ironically Elizabeth, who is far from being an infallible teacher, takes the opposite side in this argument from that she is to take in practice afterwards—here she defends Bingley's "merit" in his readiness "to yield readily—easily—to the *persuasion* of a friend," whereas later she is to be indignant that Darcy makes him do just that.

The second aspect of Darcy's character that Elizabeth probes at Netherfield is what she calls, when he admits, "my good opinion once lost is lost for ever," his "implacable resentment." Here the practical test Elizabeth administers is Wickham, against whom she believes that that resentment has been unjustly vented. Unjustifiable influence over his friend, and brutal persecution of his enemy: these are the two offences she accuses Darcy of in the first proposal scene. She has examined him as a candidate for her hand, and she fails him resoundingly. Having failed the *viva*, Darcy voluntarily sits a written exam—his letter—not to qualify himself for the same position, but to justify himself as a man of right conduct. This paper is enough to teach the teacher how wrong she has been, how "blind, partial, prejudiced, absurd."

"How despicably have I acted!" she cried. — "I, who have prided myself on my discernment! — I, who have valued myself on my abilities! . . . I have courted prepossession and ignorance, and driven reason away, where either were concerned. Till this moment, I never knew myself."

It is a salutary lesson for one who has been more fond of detecting shortcomings in others than in herself.

Darcy is to be further exonerated from the charge of implacable resentment by his remarkably forbearing behaviour to Elizabeth herself, who certainly gives provocation for resentment: after she quarrels with him in the dance, his feelings for her "soon procured her pardon"; and though his letter after her insulting refusal begins in bitterness, "the adieu is charity itself." He has been tested by having had a lot to put up with; and he has been admirably tolerant and forgiving.

However, on the third issue Darcy has more to learn, and does not acquit himself creditably until the last part of the novel. It is not a question of conduct or principle, but of manners. Again the matter is playfully canvassed between them in conversation — as usual, with an audience at hand — this time at the piano at Rosings. Elizabeth threatens to tell Colonel Fitzwilliam of Darcy's misdemeanours in Hertfordshire:

"You shall hear then — but prepare yourself for something very dreadful. The first time of my ever seeing him in Hertfordshire, you must know, was at a ball — and at this ball, what do you think he did? He danced only four dances! I am sorry to pain you — but so it was. He danced only four dances, though gentlemen were scarce; and, to my certain knowledge, more than one young lady was sitting down in want of a partner. Mr. Darcy, you cannot deny the fact.". . .

"I certainly have not the talent which some people possess," said Darcy, "of conversing easily with those I have never seen before. I cannot catch their tone of conversation, or appear interested in their concerns, as I often see done."

"My fingers," said Elizabeth, "do not move over this instrument in the masterly manner which I see so many women's do. They have not the same force or rapidity, and do not produce the same expression. But then I have always supposed it to be my own fault — because I would not take the trouble of practising. It is not that I do not believe *my* fingers as capable as any other woman's of superior execution."

Elizabeth's shortcomings as a pedagogue are still apparent in the continuing operation of that initial incident at the Meryton assembly that wounded her vanity, but here in essence she is right. Her analogy is apt — she lets Darcy know that gracious manners are not acquired simply as a ready-made gift from heaven, but that they are a skill, to be developed like other skills by exertion and practice. But Darcy, though he accepts her analogy, misapplies it and so doesn't profit from her instruction: "You are perfectly right," he acknowledges, ". . . No one admitted to the privilege of hearing you, can think any thing wanting. We neither of us perform to strangers." But piano-playing is an accomplishment that anyone may choose or not choose to develop; gracious manners are a duty that everyone must practise, and most particularly those with Darcy's prominent position in the world. Again, it takes a practical issue to make the point. Darcy's churlish first proposal brings a fierce rebuke which this time sinks in, so that he can even quote it months afterwards: "Your reproof, so well applied, I shall never forget: 'had you behaved in a more gentleman-like manner.' Those were your words." In the interval, like a good pupil, he has made a conscious effort "to correct my temper," and he displays his newly acquired skill when they meet at Pemberley:

> "My object *then*," replied Darcy, "was to shew you, by every civility in my power, that I was not so mean as to resent the past; and I hoped to obtain your forgiveness, to lessen your ill opinion, by letting you see that your reproofs had been attended to."

In this matter he has acknowledged his shortcomings and studied to correct them; and he has been an apt scholar: "You taught me a lesson," he acknowledges fervently. Like Benedick, he has resolved, "I must not seem proud. Happy are they that hear their detractions and can put them to mending" (bk. 2, chap. 3).

Elizabeth has had plenty to learn too, but Darcy, though he is the occasion of her increased self-knowledge, is not so clearly the agent. The theoretical discussions at Netherfield and Rosings, which are subsequently so neatly put to the test, are about Darcy's behaviour, not Elizabeth's. Hers have been the faults of the examiner who has overestimated her qualifications and totally misjudged her examinees. They are faults not of conduct but of judgment; so that in the process whereby her failing candidate proves himself eminently qualified, and her favoured student does the reverse, she has come to know her shortcomings and herself.

On the question of Wickham's wrongs and Darcy's supposedly implacable resentment, she was entirely misguided, and Darcy had no fault to correct; and on the first issue canvassed between them, his influence on Bingley, she has learned that it is wrong only if exerted in the wrong direction; she ceases to be fanatical in her views here, but it is an issue that will arise again for playful debate between them. Darcy does still unblushingly keep Bingley under strict if friendly surveillance, and Bingley dares propose to Jane only with Darcy's permission:

> Elizabeth longed to observe that Mr. Bingley had been a most delightful friend; so easily guided that his worth was invaluable; but she checked herself. She remembered that he had yet to learn to be laught at, and it was rather too early to begin.

That is a charming little preview of their marriage, confirming Elizabeth's conviction that "It was an union that must have been to the advantage of both." Elizabeth, by the time they are engaged, has learned some tact and forbearance in the exercise of her wit; and Darcy, having learned manners, must go on learning — he must learn to be laughed at.

The Dramatic Dilemma

Gene W. Ruoff

> Elizabeth's spirits soon rising to playfulness again, she wanted Mr. Darcy to account for his
> ever having fallen in love with her. "How could you begin?" said she. "I can comprehend your
> going on charmingly, when you had once made a beginning; but what could set you off in the
> first place?"
>
> "I cannot fix on the hour, or the spot, or the look, or the words, which laid the foundation. It
> is too long ago. I was in the middle before I knew that I had begun."
>
> —Pride and Prejudice, vol. 3, chap. 18

Of all the major narratives of the Romantic period, *Pride and Prejudice* might seem
most certain of its beginnings. It moves from a wry "truth" directly into an ini-
tiatory action: a conversation between Mr. and Mrs. Bennet provides necessary
exposition, establishes the thematic center of the novel, reveals their respective
characters, and anticipates the substantial action that will set the plot in motion,
the movement of Bingley and his entourage to Netherfield Park. That action is
only the first of what is to become a system of actions in the opening volume of
the novel, as a small and unproductively static country neighborhood is subjected
to a series of incursions — by the family and friends of Bingley, the wondrous Mr.
Collins, and Wickham and a regiment of redcoats. Volume 2 follows this pattern
of predominantly male incursions by a balancing system of female excursions:
Jane to London, Lydia to Brighton, Elizabeth first to Rosings and then virtually
to the gates of Pemberley. Volume 3 begins with Elizabeth's arrival at her true
home before breaking down into a frantic series of departures and returns:
Elizabeth back to comfort her family as Lydia and Wickham are off to God
knows where, Mr. Bennet off to join Mr. Gardiner in the search, Darcy's where-
abouts unknown in the central portion of the volume, and finally Mr. Bennet back,
Lydia and Wickham home in simpering triumph, a surprise visit by Lady

From *The Wordsworth Circle* 10, no. 1 (Winter 1979). © 1979 by Marilyn Gaull.

Catherine, and initially puzzling reappearances by Darcy and Bingley. The dizzying motion ends at last with a satisfying definitive resettlement, characters in their places with appropriately ordered motion established among them.

Aristotle would have been pleased by the formal unity of the work. Elizabeth's recognition scene is simultaneous with the reversal of her intentions, and her recognition arises directly from the action itself. The way in which the simple plot involving Jane and Bingley subtly highlights the complex plot involving Elizabeth and Darcy might even have changed his mind about double plots. Principally, though, Aristotle would have delighted in Jane Austen's skill in imitating a complete action rather than chronicling a life. More formalist studies of classic stature have been generated by *Pride and Prejudice* than by any other of her novels. In addition to the valuable commentaries of Mary Lascelles, Dorothy Van Ghent, and Reuben A. Brower, Karl Kroeber has recently pointed out how thoroughly self-sustaining the novel is, considered solely as a verbal structure. As little new remains to be said about the unity of the work, I offer only a few observations on its temporal self-containment and some of its aesthetic consequences, justified by the rather obvious fact that the formal triumph of *Pride and Prejudice* is one that Jane Austen did not choose to repeat.

Our sense of the classical tautness of *Pride and Prejudice* is enhanced, perhaps even distorted, by our knowledge of what came before and after it. *Northanger Abbey* and *Sense and Sensibility* had begun in exposition, the one exploring the deficiencies of Catherine Morland as a sentimental heroine, the other establishing in its first two chapters the economic degradation of the family of the late Henry Dashwood, which engenders the removal of Mrs. Dashwood and her daughters from Norland to Barton Cottage. *Pride and Prejudice* could easily have followed either narrative pattern, beginning with the prehistories of either Elizabeth or the Bennet family. Instead, Jane Austen chose to begin with an action, which I have discussed already, filtering in necessary exposition as her story progressed. Surprisingly little exposition is necessary, much of that devoted simply to clarifying the positions of the various families in the social hierarchy. The only significant events that antedate the central action of the novel revolve around the relationship of Wickham to the Darcy family, and the bulk even of this exposition is dramatized, either through Wickham's skewed oral history or through Darcy's letter to Elizabeth. This complication and clarification is simplicity itself compared with the untangling necessary to unearth the buried secrets that explain the convoluted actions and characters of Edward Ferrars, Colonel Brandon, and Willoughby.

Most importantly, no past action by Elizabeth, our center of interest in *Pride and Prejudice,* materially affects the plot of the novel. Indeed, Elizabeth seems in some peculiar fashion to have been born yesterday. We are led to believe, for example, that an intimate friendship has prevailed between Elizabeth and Charlotte Lucas, young ladies of twenty and twenty-seven, who live in a society that is obsessed by matrimony. Yet the scene in which Elizabeth and Charlotte weigh the prospects of a match between Jane and Bingley is barren of any suggestion that they have ever before shared their perspectives on marriage. Ideas and attitudes are dramatized — the prevailing tendency throughout the novel — but credibility is risked. After Charlotte has accepted the proposal of Mr. Collins, Jane Austen covers some of her tracks. Elizabeth reflects, "She had always felt that Charlotte's opinion of matrimony was not exactly like her own, but she could not have supposed it possible that when called into action, she would have sacrificed every better feeling to worldly advantage." That *always* is asked to do a lot of work. Striving for full dramatization in *Pride and Prejudice,* Jane Austen takes on the aesthetic problems that afflict a playwright. We all know those wooden speeches in which a friend has to explain to a friend that they are indeed friends, that they both have parents, that they haven't seen one another in over a year, and so forth. And we are only too familiar with the excesses that proceed from the textbookish demand that fiction be dramatized, such as the timeless (and mindless) scene in which, in order that a character's appearance may be described, he must gaze deeply in the mirror, contemplating the brilliant blue depths of his eyes, his pectoral development, and — increasingly of late — salient details of his lower anatomy. Even though Jane Austen is happily incapable of such atrocities, her narrative displays some of the tensions that inevitably result when fiction invokes the dramatic model.

The aesthetic dilemma that underlies *Pride and Prejudice* is best revealed in the scenes that are the turning point of the narrative, Darcy's first proposal and Elizabeth's reading of his letter of the following day. The proposal itself gives us Jane Austen the dramatist, who thrives on conflict. After Darcy has burst forth with his declaration of love, we watch as his subsequent expression of his misgivings about the alliance polarizes Elizabeth's feelings until, having controlled herself "to answer him with patience," she delivers her chillingly analytical rejection. The fun of the scene increases with the polarization, until the verbal battle that ensues threatens to render unthinkable any further communication, to say nothing of understanding. Such a scene, so readily transferable to the stage, illustrates Jane Austen's dramatic dimension, noted by A. C. Bradley and underlined recently in Donald Greene's gorgeous debunking of the myth of limitation.

This vigorous action is followed by a movement to meditation that is simply impossible dramatically. Darcy writes a letter; the act has meaning because we have, with Miss Bingley's assistance, watched him write one before. We know it as a considered action — painstaking, reflective, precise. The scene in which Elizabeth reads and rereads this letter is at the center of the principle of change within the novel, and change occurs not through action but through reflection. The scene is one of the great triumphs of English fiction because in it we visibly watch a character grow. Elizabeth is forced to rehearse the action of the novel to this point, weighing and pondering it, reconsidering her evaluations of others and, as importantly, her means of evaluation. All along she has not been just the narrational center of the novel: she has been acting consciously as a storyteller — assessing character, studying interconnections among characters, imagining underlying realities from observable actions. And the plot she has created has been wrong. As she is forced to remember the story to date, the gulf between actions as remembered and actions as observed becomes mortifying. Wickham's gross inconsistencies are patently obvious in retrospect. Like Wordsworth in *The Prelude* she has had to begin her story again: the turning point of the action is a new beginning, which is made possible by a period of extended reflection.

Such a formal disjunction between contiguous scenes — one in which a lot goes on but nothing significant happens, the other in which nothing observable happens but everything permanently important does — surely illustrates priorities of a work, and the priorities of this novel are not finally dramatic. Action separates while reflection unites. *Pride and Prejudice* is very nearly two works interleaved: a novel of action in which the causal chain, if occasionally obscure, is unbroken, and a novel of feeling in which changes of attitude and personal growth are often inversely related to the action. Darcy's major growth occurs offstage in the wake of Lydia's elopement, when he is both lost to the reader's view and, so far as she can tell, irreversibly lost to Elizabeth. Consequently, when we reach the conversation between Elizabeth and Darcy with which I prefaced this section, the question is perfectly real. Even after all the clarifications have been made, Elizabeth still does not know the beginning of Darcy's love for her, and he cannot tell her. He was in the middle before he knew he had begun. A little earlier, in answering Jane's identical question, Elizabeth had playfully spoofed the idea of a beginning of her own love: " 'It has been coming on so gradually, that I hardly know when it began. But I believe I must date it from my first seeing his beautiful grounds at Pemberley.'" A novel about love, formed on the strictest dramatic principles and employing a beautifully articulated causal plot, cannot tell us when its hero and heroine fell in love. It is a strange hybrid, using and perfecting traditional narrative forms while it heartily distrusts them. The author's ability to have it both ways is a grand achievement. But again, Jane Austen did not repeat it.

Authorial Voice
and the Total Perspective

Julia Prewitt Brown

Certain moments in literature always surprise us, no matter how many times we encounter them. One such moment is Cordelia's response to Lear, "Nothing," in the first act of the tragedy. Another is the opening sentence of *Pride and Prejudice:* "It is a truth universally acknowledged, that a single man in possession of a good fortune must be in want of a wife." Like Cordelia's unexpected reply, Austen's claim is surprising because we do not know how to interpret it. Is Cordelia's answer faint or firm, resigned or defiant? In the atmosphere of Lear's complex vanities, its stark simplicity makes it ambiguous. Similarly, the opening claim of *Pride and Prejudice* is either an instance of unalloyed irony or comic hyperbole. Read ironically, it means a great deal more than it says; read comically, it means a great deal less. Because its targets are unknown, its assurance is baffling. No matter how we read it, its finality is its irony (or comedy); it holds its "truth" and the resistance to its truth in one—the quintessential stance of the ironic comedies.

Such instances are very few and brief in Jane Austen. They constitute a direct address from the author to the reader. They dazzle us partly because they are infrequent, and they provide in their flashing ambiguity a highly concentrated version of the novelist's perspective. The discourse of the rest of *Pride and Prejudice* issues from this initial stance and falls into two broad categories, narrative and dialogue. Perceived together, as they are meant to be perceived, the narrative and the dialogue achieve the same brilliant ambiguity of the authorial voice. Consider the first appearance of narrative comment in the novel, at the close of chapter 1:

From *Jane Austen's Novels: Social Change and Literary Form.* © 1979 by the President and Fellows of Harvard College. Harvard University Press, 1979.

53

> Mr. Bennet was so odd a mixture of quick parts, sarcastic humour, reserve, and caprice, that the experience of three and twenty years had been insufficient to make his wife understand his character. *Her* mind was less difficult to develope. She was a woman of mean understanding, little information, and uncertain temper. When she was discontented she fancied herself nervous. The business of her life was to get her daughters married; its solace was visiting and news.

Considered in isolation, the passage seems objective, informative, and unambiguous. Yet when read as the conclusion of the following dialogue, the passage achieves a different resonance:

> "My dear Mr. Bennet," said his lady to him one day, "have you heard that Netherfield is let at last?" Mr. Bennet replied that he had not.
> "But it is," returned she; "for Mrs. Long has just been here, and she told me all about it."
> Mr. Bennet made no answer.
> "Do not you want to know who has taken it?" cried his wife impatiently.
> "*You* want to tell me, and I have no objection to hearing it."
> This was invitation enough.

Here we have a world of opinion and report, and one in which the effect of an event takes the place of the event itself. Neither time nor place is specified except as "day" and "neighborhood." We have only the disembodied voices of wife and husband clashing in an empty space, and ricocheting back in the form of countless amplifying ironies to the novel's opening statement. The sensibility of the dialogue is ephemeral, irrational, opinionated; it is a precarious world indeed to be followed by such stable, definitive evaluations as "She was a woman of mean understanding" or such simplistic understatements as "Her mind was less difficult to develope." This ostensibly objective narrative voice is true as far as it goes. It is true because its evaluations are, as evaluations, correct and useful. They are the necessary simplifications we live by, and the Bennets live by, for the paragraph reveals each as seen by the other.

Yet these evaluations cannot be mistaken for life itself, and Jane Austen knows they cannot. When Elizabeth returns from visiting Mr. and Mrs. Collins and her mother asks whether they "do not often talk of having Longbourn when your father is dead," we are surprised. We are required once again to acknowledge the audacity and variety and complexity of this woman's "mean understanding." The cadence of moral rationalism, the abstract, judgmental sensibility revealed in such statements as "mean understanding, little information, and uncertain temper" are always checked by action and dialogue. Through the careful juxtaposition of narrative and dialogue, Austen prevents us from investing everything in such statements.

Elizabeth too must learn that simplifications are dangerous; both she and Darcy insist on what is only provisional and half-true as final. Of her complacent division of humanity into intricate and simple characters, for example, Elizabeth comes to say, "The more I see of the world, the more am I dissatisfied with it; and every day confirms me of the inconsistency of all human characters, and of the little dependence that can be placed on the appearance of either merit or sense." The irony of the novel's opening sentence lies in its assurance in simplification and generalization, its insistence that the local perception is universal, absolute, permanent. We simplify our world in order to live in it; and Austen (like Sterne) keeps telling us we do. *Pride and Prejudice* is an exhilarating work because it turns us back continually on life by showing us the failure of language and the individual mind to capture life's unexpectedness. And beneath the exhilaration lies an affection for the bizarre actuality of things. The opening hyperbole, for example, contains an element of eccentric delight in human exaggeration.

The narrative voice, then, provides some limit, some barrier, which the action strives ceaselessly (and successfully) to overcome. The narrator's provision of certitude, despite its accuracy, is temporary. Nevertheless, its role in the novel is of vital importance. Indeed, without the narrative voice, the moral structure of the novel would crumble. The terms of order in the novel are defined by the narrative voice, just as the terms of anarchy are defined by dialogue and action. In this respect, Austen works in a way similar to that of George Eliot. Eliot's compassionate narrative voice is used both to reprimand and to redeem the failing world of Middlemarch. Austen's rational narrative voice is used both to abuse and applaud the evasions of humankind—abuse the cruelties and applaud the abundance. Only through the careful and complex juxtaposition of action and narrative does each author maintain her ambiguity. The depth of both *Pride and Prejudice* and *Middlemarch* depends on the reader's sensitivity to the relationship between the action of the characters and the voice that enfolds it. As James wrote, we cannot speak of incident and narration as though they were mutually exclusive:

> I cannot . . . conceive in any novel worth discussing, of a passage of description that is not in its intention narrative, a passage of dialogue that is not in its intention descriptive, a touch of truth of any sort that does not partake of the nature of incident, or an incident that derives its interest from any other source than the general and

only source of the success of a work of art — that of being illustrative
. . . I cannot see what is meant by talking as if there were a part of
the novel which is the story and a part which for mystical reasons is
not.

In Austen, the "story" is made meaningful by narrative intrusion; and "description" or reflection is made meaningful by story.

Jane Austen's narrative voice establishes a stability in a world of fluctuating
opinions and exaggerations. The opening page of chapter 2, for example, dwells
on the various "reports" of Bingley and of the party he will bring with him.
Bingley is "wonderfully handsome" and "extremely agreeable," and he is bringing "twelve ladies and seven gentlemen" to the next assembly with him. In conclusion (and not wholly in defiance) of these reports, the narrator comments:
"[The party] consisted of only five altogether; Mr. Bingley, his two sisters, the
husband of the eldest, and another young man . . . Mr. Bingley was good
looking and gentlemanlike; he had a pleasant countenance, and easy, unaffected
manners." This pattern is characteristic in Jane Austen: the responses to an event
are catalogued, beginning with the most exaggerated and concluding with the
true fact of the case, or the truest response.

The Bennet family's response to Mr. Collins's engagement to Charlotte
Lucas is another example of this progress toward truth. Sir William Lucas comes
to Longbourn bearing the news, and the first reactions are attributed to the least
rational of the group: "Mrs. Bennet, with more perseverance than politeness,
protested he must be entirely mistaken, and Lydia, always unguarded and often
uncivil, boisterously exclaimed, 'Good Lord! Sir William, how can you tell such
a story? — Do you not know that Mr. Collins wants to marry Lizzy?'" After Sir
William's departure, the responses flow with enthusiasm, beginning once again
with Mrs. Bennet and Lydia, to Mr. Bennet, Jane, and finally Elizabeth, whose
simple statement truly evaluates the event with regard to her friendship with
Charlotte. "Elizabeth felt persuaded that no real confidence could ever subsist between them again." This pattern, with its suggestion of the endless variations
and subterfuge surrounding an event, implies a belief in the difficult accessibility,
perhaps the inaccessibility, of truth. The reliable interpretation of a chapter or incident is usually founded on the response or evaluation stated last.

The conclusions to the ironic comedies are especially ambiguous in this
respect. Each has its own ironic touch, each calls to mind the memory of some
incident of absurdity or insensibility and in so doing, gently undermines the con-
spicuous gaiety of the marriage union. The allusion to an imperfection is often
injected in the penultimate lines of the last chapter (Lady Catherine's visit to
Pemberley, Mrs. Elton's opinion of Emma's wedding clothes) just before the

perfect happiness of the union is proclaimed. It is as if the modes of resistance to the truth become part of the truth itself.

The paradox of truth and truth's compromise accounts for the paradoxical mood of uncomfortable harmony with which most of the novels close. Emma's "perfect happiness" and Anne Elliot's "perfect felicity" have the slightly unsettling effect of flattery. Emma is still not above making fun of Robert Martin, as she does in a closing dialogue with Mr. Knightley, and Anne Elliot assures herself that she was right to reject Wentworth in the first place. In a world that the novels themselves have so insistently pronounced to be relative, how can we accept the absolute assertions of the endings? Their ambiguity is intended and is a way of pointing out life's compromise of felicity without derogating what felicity remains. By the time we reach the conclusion of *Pride and Prejudice* we understand the limitations of such words as "perfect" and know how to interpret them; when we close the pages of *Emma* we have learned enough about Emma and Mr. Knightley and Highbury and life in general there to know exactly how much perfection and how much happiness are included in the narrator's "perfect happiness."

The narrative voice, then, possesses the essential perspective of the novel. Although Austen's style has been compared to that of Henry James, her use of a vigorous and daunting narrative voice distinguishes them. This voice has more in common with that of the George Eliot narrator, whose all-inclusive compassion envelops the divisions and decay of the story, or that of the Fielding narrator, whose humor is equally tolerant. Austen's authorial consciousness is also binding, for it accepts in its embrace the evasions and irrationalities of direct dialogue and the cool, clear cadence of reason of the objective narrative. It brings them together in its brief flashes of genius, such as in the opening sentence of *Pride and Prejudice.* In such moments, the two streams of discourse in Jane Austen, narration and dialogue, rush together completely. They represent the *effect* of the novel, the total perspective we are to gain, one that rises spontaneously out of the interaction between narration and dialogue.

It may seem to belie Austen's morality to insist that the evasions and even cruelties that arise from the insensibility or partial insight of the characters of *Pride and Prejudice* are somehow sanctioned by the author. Yet the acceptance of such things is securely encompassed in her wisdom, just as Lady Catherine is finally received at Pemberley. And often, particularly in the ironic comedies, the modes of resistance to what is right or true are fairly innocent. The desire to make Bingley more handsome than he really is, to make his party larger than it really is, reveals a need to make ordinary life more glamorous and drastic than it really is. Emma's requirement that life in Highbury be more vivid, elegant, and mysterious than it is reveals a similar need. It is one of the paradoxes of Austen's perspective that such requirements are both ferocious and innocent.

Pride and Prejudice, however, deals less with the problem of accepting an inelegant and unpoetic world than with accepting an irrational and absurd one. If Emma's aspirations are for more witty and more alive surroundings, Elizabeth's efforts are to restrain the anarchic energies of cynicism and insensibility in her parents. The unrelenting invasion of sense by nonsense, of sensibility by moral nullity, of humor by nihilism is a dominant theme in the novel. And determining the proper moral posture to adopt in such a world is the dilemma of individuality.

Pride and Prejudice: Structure and Social Vision

David Monaghan

Courtship is relegated to the periphery of *Sense and Sensibility,* but it reassumes a very central position in *Pride and Prejudice.* The subject is introduced by the novel's famous opening sentence: "It is a truth universally acknowledged, that a single man in possession of a good fortune, must be in want of a wife." And it remains in the forefront throughout the first chapter which is given over entirely to Mrs. Bennet, "the business of [whose] life was to get her daughters married." The novel's major plot threads are set in motion by the arrival of four strangers in the village of Meryton, and the fabric is not completed until each is married — Darcy to Elizabeth Bennet, Bingley to Jane Bennet, Wickham to Lydia Bennet, and Mr. Collins to Charlotte Lucas. The choosing of partners is not simple, however, and seven unsuccessful courtships litter the path to the altar. Mr. Collins is rejected by Elizabeth; Wickham tries to elope with Georgiana Darcy, pays attention to Miss King, and becomes briefly involved with Elizabeth; Elizabeth and Colonel Fitzwilliam are prevented from pursuing a mutual attraction by financial considerations; Darcy is involved with Caroline Bingley, and, at least in Lady Catherine de Bourgh's mind, is the suitor of Anne de Bourgh. At the centre of this web of courtships is that of Darcy and Elizabeth, for it is through the development of their relationship that the novel makes its main statement. The other love affairs are subordinate and their function is largely exhausted once they have fulfilled the role of expanding or modifying the issues raised between hero and heroine.

In Jane Austen's novels difficulties between hero and heroine are usually created, and their final union delayed, by the immaturity that one or both of

From *Jane Austen: Structure and Social Vision.* © 1980 by David Monaghan. The Macmillan Press, 1980.

them brings into their relationship. In *Northanger Abbey, Sense and Sensibility,* and *Emma,* the heroines are deficient; Catherine Morland lacks discrimination, Marianne Dashwood has an inflated sense of her innate abilities, and Emma is an "imaginist." In *Persuasion,* on the other hand, it is the faults of the hero that cause problems because Wentworth allows his judgement to be clouded by feelings of resentment. And in *Mansfield Park,* both Fanny Price and Edmund Bertram are inadequate, she being too reticent and he too easily taken in by charm. *Pride and Prejudice,* however, does not obviously conform to this pattern, in that both Darcy and Elizabeth Bennet are extremely mature people by the time that they meet. The mediocrity of her environment has made Elizabeth think too well of her admittedly excellent intelligence, but otherwise she has few personal flaws and many virtues. Amongst the most notable of these is the "quickness of observation" which enables her to see through the Bingley sisters' charming facade. They possess "the power of being agreeable," but Elizabeth almost immediately recognises that they are "proud and conceited." Elizabeth is also morally sound. This is particularly evident in her thoughts about marriage, which are characterised by a concern with establishing a proper relationship between the demands of personal feeling and the need for financial security. And furthermore, Elizabeth can mount a social performance that is brilliant and daring but always proper. Her arrival at Netherfield, for example, flushed and muddy after a three-mile walk across the fields, is unorthodox, but is perfectly appropriate to the needs of the situation created by her sister's illness. Darcy, too, has many good qualities. As master of Pemberley, he acts in accordance with the highest moral standards; his intelligence is sharp enough to cut straight through Bingley's vague logic; his manners are dignified if rather too reserved; and he possesses excellent judgement —Caroline Bingley's elegant posturings, for instance, come no closer to deceiving Darcy than they do Elizabeth Bennet.

Yet if we knew Darcy and Elizabeth only through their encounters with each other, we would never suspect that they were so mature. Elizabeth completely and wilfully misjudges Darcy's character, overlooks Wickham's faults simply because he is Darcy's enemy, and behaves towards Darcy with something approaching real insolence. Darcy is no better. At the Meryton ball he rudely rejects Bingley's proposal that he dance with Elizabeth. Later, he treats Mrs. Bennet with obvious scorn, joins in the Bingley sisters' cruel gossip about the Bennet family, and finally proposes to Elizabeth in a way that suggests he feels almost as much loathing as love. This uncharacteristic immaturity can be explained by the fact that, although each is fairly knowing in the ways of his own social circle, neither has an accurate sense of the other's. Elizabeth Bennet is firmly located in a world of lesser gentry and bourgeoisie. Her father owns a small estate worth £2000 per annum, her mother is the daughter of an attorney, and her uncle, Mr.

Gardiner, is in trade. Darcy, on the other hand, belongs to the noble de Bourgh family, possesses the Pemberley estate, and has an income of £10,000 per annum, enough to put his among the four hundred most important families. Lacking any experience of the other's world, each relies on stereotypes; Elizabeth accepts the common view that aristocrats are worthless snobs, and Darcy believes that anyone connected with trade must be vulgar and unworthy of respect. Unfortunately, since Darcy's visit to Meryton brings him into contact with Mrs. Bennet, and since Elizabeth witnesses Darcy's supercilious behaviour at the Meryton ball, their first exposure to each other's worlds serves to confirm rather than disprove these stereotypes.

Further acquaintance gives Darcy and Elizabeth opportunities to refine their crude social typecasting. And Darcy does indeed quickly come to see some of Elizabeth's virtues. However, instead of reexamining her milieu in the light of the fact that it has produced at least one admirable person, he simply tries to isolate Elizabeth from her background. In his dealings with Elizabeth, Darcy begins to behave politely, but he continues to express contempt for the Bennet family and the people of Meryton. By so doing, Darcy provides Elizabeth with plenty of evidence to confirm her prejudices. However, the way in which Elizabeth reacts to Darcy suggests that her feelings towards him have their origins in more than simple moral disapproval. Even at his worst Darcy is no more objectionable than Lady Catherine de Bourgh or Mr. Collins, and he is certainly not as bad as Wickham is finally revealed to be. Yet, for all her awareness of the faults of these people, Elizabeth is never rude to them. When it is necessary to let Wickham know that she has discovered the reality of his relationship with the Darcy family, Elizabeth does so with kindness and tact, and ends on a placatory note: "Come, Mr. Wickham, we are brother and sister, you know. Do not let us quarrel about the past. In future, I hope we shall be always of one mind." Darcy's attempts to engage Elizabeth in conversations or dance, on the other hand, are greeted with ever more rude rebuffs. This kind of behaviour is so uncharacteristic of Elizabeth that we must assume that it has deep emotional roots. And, indeed, it seems likely that it derives from an unconscious need to deny that, for all his faults, she finds Darcy attractive. Up to this point in her life Elizabeth's emotional equilibrium has never been seriously challenged. Throughout her relationship with Wickham, for example, she is always extremely aware of how she feels, and can even discuss his defection to Miss King in a calm and analytical way: "I am now convinced, my dear aunt, that I have never been much in love; for had I really experienced that pure and elevating passion, I should at present detest his very name, and wish him all manner of evil." Therefore, it is not at all surprising that she should meet the threat Darcy poses by making every effort to drive him away, even though to do this she must repeatedly transgress the bounds of politeness.

Darcy is not put off by Elizabeth's rudeness, and in fact seems to sense the emotions that lie beneath it. As he explains later, her behaviour was such as to make him anticipate the success of his first marriage proposal, and Elizabeth acknowledges the ambiguity of her response to him:

"I believed you to be wishing, expecting my addresses."
"My manners must have been in fault, but not intentionally I assure you."

Therefore, in spite of his reservations about her background, Darcy makes many attempts to approach Elizabeth. Each time, Elizabeth rejects him. This creates an extremely frustrating situation and it is one that cannot be resolved until each has come to a better understanding of the other's social group. For all the attentions he pays her, Darcy will be unacceptable to Elizabeth so long as he fails to recognise that the gentry-middle class as a whole is worthy of his respect. And Elizabeth will continue to blind herself to Darcy's virtues until she has arrived at a fair estimation of the environment which has shaped him. Darcy's meeting with the excellent Gardiners, whose gentility is not diminished by the fact that they live within sight of their warehouses, and Elizabeth's introduction to Pemberley, a place that epitomises the taste, importance, and enormous social responsibilities of the nobility, are necessary prerequisites of personal reconciliation.

The social and the personal are so closely bound together in the relationship between Elizabeth and Darcy that the larger implications of the marriage into which they finally enter are very evident. In her other novels Jane Austen tends to suggest that the continued moral well-being of society depends on the ability of the gentry to ward off the disruptive influence of the middle class and the aristocracy. But *Pride and Prejudice* concludes with a union which grows directly out of the ability of the participants to recognise that, in spite of their different functions, the middle class, the gentry, and the nobility are all committed to the ideal of concern for others. The materialism and vulgarity of the bourgeoisie are as much in evidence in *Pride and Prejudice* as they were in *Northanger Abbey* and *Sense and Sensibility*. So is the snobbery of the aristocracy. But here people like Charlotte Lucas and Lady Catherine de Bourgh represent deviations from the norm of their groups rather than the norm itself.

Since courtship contributes so much to the themes of *Pride and Prejudice*, it is appropriate that dancing, which is, as Henry Tilney points out, the courtship ritual *par excellence*, should play a major part in its structure. Four incidents involving invitations to dance lay the groundwork for a pattern of approach and rejection which serves as an emblem of Darcy's relationship with Elizabeth. Other dance invitations—Bingley's to Jane, Collins's to Elizabeth, and Wickham's to Elizabeth—provide a commentary on the problems and misunder standings that exist between Darcy and Elizabeth. The dance disappears from the novel after the Netherfield ball, and emphasis is transferred to the visit. By comparing her impressions of Rosings and Pemberley Elizabeth is finally able to achieve a proper understanding of the aristocracy. Darcy's perspective on the middle class is similarly broadened by his meetings with Mr. Collins and Sir William Lucas at Rosings, and the Gardiners at Pemberley. Consequently the pattern of approach and rejection which was continued at Rosings is broken at Pemberley when Elizabeth accepts several invitations in rapid succession. These temporary polite unions promise something more permanent, and the final section of *Pride and Prejudice* is organised around three marriages, those between Lydia and Wickham, and Bingley and Jane, quite literally clearing the way for Darcy and Elizabeth's.

Pride and Prejudice is much cleaner in its structural lines than either *Northanger Abbey* or *Sense and Sensibility.* In both of these novels patterns have to be extricated from an often confusing plethora of formal social occasions, and in *Sense and Sensibility* come nowhere near to providing an adequate vehicle for all its themes. *Pride and Prejudice,* on the other hand, readily divides into three sections, each controlled by a different and thematically appropriate social ritual — dancing for the problems of courtship, the visit for the broadening of social horizons, and marriage for the resolution of conflicts. It is not in its patterning alone, however, that *Pride and Prejudice* reveals Jane Austen's increasing sense of the possibilities of the formal social occasion. The Netherfield ball scene surpasses anything to be found in the earlier novels because it not only plays its part in the dance invitation motif, but also serves as a microcosm of the relationships and issues developed in the first section of the novel. This use of the extended scene prefigures the complex individual formal social occasions we find in *Mansfield Park* and *Emma,* such as the Sotherton excursion, the theatricals, the Crown ball, and the trip to Donwell.

The connection between marriage and dancing is rarely more obvious than in the early pages of *Pride and Prejudice,* for the arrival of a new tenant at Netherfield causes Mrs. Bennet and her younger daughters to talk of little else. Partners for the evening and partners for life become almost indistinguishable as Mrs. Bennet's mind rushes on anxiously towards matrimony:

> To be fond of dancing was a certain step towards falling in love; and very lively hopes of Mr. Bingley's heart were entertained.
> "If I can but see one of my daughters happily settled at Netherfield," said Mrs. Bennet to her husband, "and all the others equally well married, I shall have nothing to wish for."

Outside of Mrs. Bennet's imagination, however, unions are not formed so easily, and Elizabeth Bennet and Darcy show little sign of becoming infected with the mating spirit. Far from considering marriage, Darcy neglects even to ask Elizabeth to dance at the Meryton Assembly, and manages to do so in a way that arouses her hostility. Because he regards Meryton society as vulgar, Darcy refuses to recognise that it can claim even the minimum of good manners from him. When Mrs. Long, who "does not keep a carriage, and had come to the ball in a hack chaise" sits next to him, Darcy maintains an offensive silence for a full thirty minutes. It is not surprising, then, that he bridles at the sociable Bingley's attempts to make him join in the dancing:

> "Which do you mean?" and turning round, he looked for a moment at Elizabeth, till catching her eye, he withdrew his own and coldly said, "She is tolerable; but not handsome enough to tempt *me;* and I am in no humour at present to give consequence to young ladies who are slighted by other men."

Further acquaintance with Elizabeth, however, soon modifies Darcy's attitude. Unattractive as he might find Meryton society in general, Darcy cannot long ignore the fact that Elizabeth is at least physically appealing: "But no sooner had he made it clear to himself and his friends that she had hardly a good feature in her face, than he began to find it was rendered uncommonly intelligent by the beautiful expression of her dark eyes." And at Sir William Lucas's party he discovers that she has more substantial virtues. The repartee in which Elizabeth engages him for eavesdropping on her conversation with Charlotte Lucas is charming, and her performance at the piano is admirable. Unlike her sister Mary, who has no sense of the limitations of her accomplishments, Elizabeth is aware that though her playing and singing are "pleasing" they are "by no means capital." Consequently, to avoid taxing the interest of her audience, she tactfully gives up her place at the piano after a song or two. Darcy is so impressed by this display of concern for others that he begins to discriminate between Elizabeth and her world. The party as a whole clearly disgusts him, and when the guests begin to dance he expresses "silent indignation at such a mode of passing the evening, to the exclusion of all conversation." Sir William Lucas's ill-timed praise of dancing persuades Darcy to give voice to his feelings:

> "There is nothing like dancing after all. — I consider it as one of the first refinements of polished societies."
> "Certainly, Sir; — and it has the advantage also of being in vogue amongst the less polished societies of the world. — Every savage can dance."

Primitive and crude as the proceedings in general may appear to Darcy's prejudiced eyes, nevertheless he has no objection to joining in when Elizabeth Bennet is offered as a partner: "'You cannot refuse to dance, I am sure, when so much beauty is before you.' And taking her hand, he would have given it to Mr. Darcy, who, though extremely surprised, was not unwilling to receive it."

Because Darcy's attitude to her society is no better than it was when he rejected Bingley's similar proposal at the Meryton ball, Elizabeth is quite justified in refusing him. However, there seems to be more to her refusal than disapproval of his behaviour in two specific situations. After the Meryton ball, Elizabeth assured her mother that she would "*never* . . . dance with him.*" This suggests that she believes she knows the man in a very final sort of way, and that the arrogance she has observed constitutes the sum total of his character. That any part of Darcy's attitude to Meryton society might be justified, or that he might have other better qualities, completely escapes her. The source of Elizabeth's confidence in her understanding of Darcy's character is made very clear by a conversation with Charlotte Lucas. Elizabeth and Charlotte have very different attitudes to Darcy's pride. However, neither sees any reason to go beyond it for an explanation of his character because each regards this quality as the essential mark of the aristocrat. Thus Charlotte argues:

> His pride . . . does not offend *me* so much as pride often does, because there is an excuse for it. One cannot wonder that so very fine a young man, with family, fortune, every thing in his favour, should think highly of himself. If I may so express it, he has a *right* to be proud.

Elizabeth, on the other hand, takes the view that because of his pride, the aristocrat is inevitably offensive in his dealings with those he considers to be his inferiors: "I could easily forgive *his* pride, if he had not mortified *mine.*" The Darcys created by Charlotte and Elizabeth bear more resemblance to the actual man than young Lucas's Squire — Westernish aristocrat, who "keep[s] a pack of foxhounds, and drink[s] a bottle of wine every day." Nevertheless, all three are essentially stereotypes, based on preconceived notions rather than on any observation of actual conduct, and as such are static figures incapable of moral growth. It is only because she views Darcy in such simplistic terms that Elizabeth can be so confident that she has complete knowledge of his character.

Elizabeth and Darcy have quickly developed an extremely frustrating relationship. He is attracted to her, but because he fails to go beyond stereotypes in approaching her milieu, and because of a combination of genuine objections to his behaviour and a similar weakness in her attitude to the aristocracy, there seems little chance that she will accept his advances. To emphasise the impasse at which Darcy and Elizabeth have arrived, Jane Austen introduces the approach and rejection movement, established by Darcy's unsuccessful dance invitation, into each of their four main formal encounters at Netherfield. The pattern is set by the events of the first evening. When Darcy tries to pay a compliment to Elizabeth, whom Miss Bingley has just described as "a great reader," by stating a preference for a woman who adds to all the usual skills and talents "something more substantial, in the improvement of her mind by extensive reading," she ignores the personal implications of his comments, and engages him in a sharp exchange about feminine accomplishments:

> "I am no longer surprised at your knowing *only* six accomplished women. I rather wonder now at your knowing *any*."
> "Are you so severe upon your own sex, as to doubt the possibility of all this?"
> "*I* never saw such a woman. *I* never saw such capacity, and taste, and application, and elegance, as you describe, united."

In that Darcy's attitude to her family and its middle-class associations has still not improved, Elizabeth is justified in rejecting his approach once again. It would, after all, be hard to expect her to be receptive to a man who just previously had commented that the possession of relatives in Cheapside "must very materially lessen their [Jane and Elizabeth's] chance of marrying men of any consideration in the world," especially as his words contrast so unfavourably with Bingley's generous comment that "if they had uncles enough to fill *all* Cheapside . . . it would not make them one jot less agreeable." Nevertheless, the way in which Elizabeth deals with Darcy is far from satisfactory, because it shows that she too is in the grip of obscuring prejudices. Darcy's comments on accomplishments are serious and intelligent. Elizabeth, however, is so obsessed with her stereotype that she simply twists his words and, by denying that women exist who can match up to his ideal, suggests that he is a snob who speaks only to assert his own superiority. Consequently, she misses an opportunity to learn that there is something more to Darcy than was apparent at the Meryton Assembly. Elizabeth's failure to acknowledge Darcy's virtues is all the more inexcusable because earlier in the evening she was given information about his background that should have enabled her to put his demands for intellectual seriousness in their proper context. During a discussion about libraries, it becomes evident that Pemberley is a place with a long tradition of respect for things of the mind, and that Darcy is striving to maintain that tradition:

> "What a delightful library you have at Pemberley, Mr. Darcy!"
> "It ought to be good," he replied, "it has been the work of many generations."
> "And then you have added so much to it yourself, you are always buying books."

"I cannot comprehend the neglect of a family library in such days as these."

Justifiable disapproval and prejudice alone, however, do not provide a sufficient explanation for the particularly virulent style in which Elizabeth rebuffs Darcy. She had just as much reason to think badly of him at Sir William Lucas's party, and yet she turned him down politely on that occasion: "Indeed, Sir, I have not the least intention of dancing. — I entreat you not to suppose that I moved this way in order to beg for a partner." Moreover, Elizabeth is never overtly rude to Lady Catherine de Bourgh, although she fits the aristocratic stereotype much better than Darcy and offers considerable provocation. Even the most outrageous of Lady Catherine's comments evoke nothing more than an amused or ironic response from Elizabeth. Neither politeness nor detachment, however, are characteristics of this Netherfield encounter with Darcy. Instead Elizabeth seems to be in the grip of strong feelings. Since the intention of Elizabeth's words is to hurt, hatred would seem to be the most likely source of her passion. However, their effect suggests something else. Instead of being offended by Elizabeth's outburst, Darcy finds it attractive. Thus when Caroline Bingley tries to take advantage of what seems a good opportunity to discredit Elizabeth, she is surprised to find her malicious comments turned against herself:

"Eliza Bennet," said Miss Bingley, when the door was closed on her, "is one of those young ladies who seek to recommend themselves to the other sex, by undervaluing their own; and with many men, I dare say, it succeeds. But, in my opinion, it is a paltry device, a very mean art."

"Undoubtedly," replied Darcy, to whom this remark was chiefly addressed, "there is meanness in *all* the arts which ladies sometimes condescend to employ for captivation. Whatever bears affinity to cunning is despicable."

For Darcy to respond in a way that amounts to a statement of preference for Elizabeth over Caroline clearly suggests that he has seen beneath the surface of Elizabeth's words. There was indeed a good deal of "mean art" in them, although its aim was the opposite of what Caroline supposes, but there was also something akin to real affection.

With the addition of this new element, the relationship between Darcy and Elizabeth becomes even more difficult, and a spiral effect is created. Evidence that Elizabeth loves him encourages Darcy to intensify his approaches. Because she is unable to deal with the feelings aroused by these approaches, Elizabeth rejects him with ever increased violence. However, the more passion Elizabeth puts into warding off Darcy, the more affection he perceives, and the greater become his efforts to establish contact with her. The spiral ascends through several turns on the second day of Elizabeth's visit to Netherfield. A conversation about Bingley's hasty style of letter-writing quickly intensifies into a more general debate about the value of precipitance. Darcy's contribution to the discussion is intended only to make a rather limited plea for the value of acting upon a consideration of circumstances and with an attention to propriety. Elizabeth, however, broadens and distorts his arguments so as to suggest that he is placing a sterile concern with form ahead of the claims of "friendship and affection." Again, then, she reacts to his conversational approach by rudely hinting that he is a snob. Darcy, though, perceives more than insults in her words, for he makes a much more direct approach later in the evening. Inspired by Miss Bingley's playing of "a lively Scotch air . . . Mr. Darcy, drawing near Elizabeth, said to her—

'Do not you feel a great inclination, Miss Bennet, to seize such an opportunity of dancing a reel?' " This invitation is presumably only a theoretical one. It is nevertheless genuine in spirit, and would not have been extended unless Darcy had been anticipating that Elizabeth would respond rather more favourably than she did at the Lucas's party. In actuality he receives his most explicit rejection so far. With extreme perversity Elizabeth chooses to interpret his proposal as a snobbish attempt to expose her bad taste, and so turns it down:

> You wanted me, I know, to say "Yes," that you might have the pleasure of despising my taste; but I always delight in overthrowing those kind of schemes, and cheating a person of their premeditated contempt. I have therefore made up my mind to tell you, that I do not want to dance a reel at all—and now despise me if you dare.

Darcy's rude treatment of Mrs. Bennet during her visit only a few hours earlier justifies Elizabeth's continued disapproval. However, it becomes increasingly evident in the course of the day that her definition of him as an utter snob is inadequate, and that by clinging to it so rigidly she is depriving herself of opportunities to achieve a richer understanding of his character. The impropriety of Mrs. Bennet's behaviour, for example, is a source of great embarrassment to Elizabeth herself: "Darcy only smiled; and the general pause which ensued made Elizabeth tremble lest her mother should be exposing herself again." Yet, she will not allow the possibility that Darcy's rudeness may have been caused by disapproval of Mrs. Bennet's actual conduct as well as by objections to her low origins. Similarly, during the evening, because of her single-minded approach to Darcy, Elizabeth blinds herself to the fact that he is a man who possesses both a serious intelligence and sufficient *joie de vivre* to cherish the idea of dancing a reel.

The spiral ascends still further on the next day. Far from being put off by the refusal of his dance invitation, Darcy finds such a mixture of "sweetness and archness in her manner" that he becomes quite "bewitched." Consequently, he responds to an attempt by Miss Bingley and Mrs. Hurst to exclude Elizabeth from a morning walk, by immediately inviting her to join in. Elizabeth, however, not only refuses, but does so in such a way as to group Darcy with the snobbish Bingley sisters: "No, no; stay where you are. — You are charmingly group'd, and appear to uncommon advantage. The picturesque would be spoilt by admitting a fourth." Elizabeth's self-deceit is blatant. Darcy had "felt [his companions'] rudeness" and had acted to correct it. Thus, rather than being the snob Elizabeth labels him, Darcy has shown himself to be a man capable of attending to the needs of others.

A similar sequence of events occurs in the evening. Caroline Bingley's efforts to attract Darcy's attention by parading up and down the room are unsuccessful until she persuades Elizabeth to join her: "Elizabeth was surprised, but agreed to it immediately. Miss Bingley succeeded no less in the real object of her civility; Mr. Darcy looked up." Elizabeth's response to Darcy's display of interest is to indulge herself in an extended mockery of his character. She dwells on his supposed intimacy with the vain Caroline Bingley, twits him for his lack of humour, suggests that he believes himself to be perfect, and concludes by again accusing him of "vanity and pride." As usual Elizabeth is so busy repelling Darcy that she ignores indications that there is more to his character than she supposes. Darcy meets her accusation that he is guilty of vanity and pride by drawing distinctions between the words: "Yes, vanity is a weakness indeed. But pride — where there is a real superiority of mind, pride will be always under good regulation." Although she has already learnt from Mary that "a person may be proud without being vain," Elizabeth chooses to believe that Darcy is simply splitting semantic hairs in order to justify his own behaviour, and "turned away to hide a smile." Yet Darcy has provided some very clear guidelines to his strengths and weaknesses. He is guilty of pride in the sense of vanity, but he also possesses that proper pride that derives from an awareness of the importance of his role in society.

Since such a firm pattern of approach and rejection has been established, it is extremely surprising that when Darcy next asks Elizabeth to dance, at the Netherfield ball, she accepts: "she found herself suddenly addressed by Mr. Darcy, who took her so much by surprise in his application for her hand, that, without knowing what she did, she accepted him." The phrase "without knowing what she did" tells us why. There are many things on Elizabeth's mind during the Netherfield ball, including disappointment at Wickham's unexpected absence, and a mixture of amusement and repugnance at the revelation of Mr. Collins's matrimonial intentions. When Darcy comes upon her, then, her conscious thoughts are elsewhere, and her feelings for once get a chance to express themselves. This does not mean, though, that Elizabeth is any closer to acknowledging her emotions. The interval between Darcy's invitation and the beginning of the dance gives her time to collect herself, and as they move down the set she makes determined efforts to reestablish some distance. First of all, she ridicules the surface formalities of the dance in order to deny its significance as a courtship ritual, and thus to deprive Darcy's invitation of its significance: "It is *your* turn to say something now, Mr. Darcy. —I talked about the dance and *you* ought to make some kind of remark on the size of the room, or the number of couples." This is sheer perversity, because Elizabeth is usually well aware of the larger implications of dancing. Certainly, when Mr. Collins engaged her for the first two dances, Elizabeth immediately realised that he was planning to make her his wife: "It now first struck her, that *she* was selected from among her sisters as worthy of being the mistress of Hunsford Parsonage." Her other tactics include comments on Darcy's "unsocial, taciturn disposition." However, it is by making repeated and unnecessary references to her knowledge of Darcy's supposed mistreatment of Wickham that Elizabeth most effectively expresses her hostility: "He has been so unlucky as to lose *your* friendship . . . and in a manner which he is likely to suffer from all his life." Temporary acceptance is thus successfully translated into a promise of permanent separation:

> "But if I do not take your likeness now, I may never have another
> opportunity."
> "I would by no means suspend any pleasure of yours," he coldly
> replied. She said no more, and they went down the other dance and
> parted in silence.

The Netherfield ball brings the first movement of *Pride and Prejudice* to an end, and Jane Austen constructs it in such a way that it sums up and comments on many of the elements in the complex of attraction and repulsion that comprises the relationship which has developed between Darcy and Elizabeth. The differences in Elizabeth's reactions to her three partners, actual and would-be, remind us, for example, that she is usually a good deal more mature than in her dealings with Darcy. Although the possibility of dancing with the attractive Wickham has filled Elizabeth's thoughts prior to the ball, she responds sensibly to the disappointing realisation that he is not present:

> But Elizabeth was not formed for ill-humour; and though every prospect
> of her own was destroyed for the evening, it could not dwell long on her
> spirits; and having told all her griefs to Charlotte Lucas . . . she was
> soon able to make a voluntary transition to the oddities of her cousin.

This epitomises the secure emotional balance that Elizabeth displays throughout her friendship with Wickham. Although she takes Wickham as "her model of the amiable and pleasing" Elizabeth does not build up their relationship into more than it is, or lose touch with the fact that her feelings for him are rather limited.

The role Elizabeth had hoped Wickham would play is usurped by Mr. Collins who claims the first two dances. It is clear to Elizabeth that Collins intends dancing to prepare the way for a marriage proposal. Matrimony is not something Elizabeth can afford to take lightly, because failure to find a husband will leave her in a state of relative poverty. And Collins is, in fact, well enough situated in life to guarantee her future security. Elizabeth's response to Collins, however, proves that she is unwilling to put self-interest ahead of principles. For her, marriage without affection and respect constitutes a sacrifice of "every better feeling to worldly advantage," and since Collins's character is so accurately reflected in his performance on the dance floor, Elizabeth separates from him without the slightest wish of extending their relationship:

> Mr. Collins, awkward and solemn, apologising instead of attending, and often moving wrong without being aware of it, gave her all the shame and misery which a disagreeable partner for a couple of dances can give. The moment of her release from him was exstacy.

While dancing with Darcy, Elizabeth, as we have already seen, shows none of this knowledge of her emotions or regard for principles, even though Darcy tries to remind her of the moral implications of the polite performance: "Are you consulting your own feelings in the present case, or do you imagine that you are gratifying mine?" Equally lacking is the good judgement with which she approaches Collins. Darcy's attempts to warn her that she is mistaken about his relationship with Wickham are supported by Jane, who has made enquiries of Bingley, and by Caroline Bingley. Yet Elizabeth finds reasons to doubt all three, and will not allow that there might be any validity in their combined claims. The "wilful ignorance" of which Elizabeth accuses Miss Bingley in this instance more accurately reflects her own refusal to see beyond a version of events that conforms with her personal prejudices.

A similar lack of good judgement is evident in Elizabeth's interpretation of Darcy's attitude to her family and relatives. The Bennets behave particularly badly during the Netherfield ball:

> To Elizabeth it appeared, that had her family made an agreement to expose themselves as much as they could during the evening, it would have been impossible for them to play their parts with more spirit, or finer success.

Mr. Collins pays Darcy sycophantic attention; Mrs. Bennet rattles on loudly about Jane's chances of marrying Bingley, and sneers at Darcy; Mary bores the guests with her weak singing; and Mr. Bennet silences her rudely. Elizabeth is acutely aware that none of this escapes Darcy's attention, and is not entirely unjustified in believing that he reacts to their foolishness in a cruel and snobbish way:

> That [Bingley's] two sisters and Mr. Darcy, however, should have such an opportunity of ridiculing her relations was bad enough, and she could not determine whether the silent contempt of the gentleman, or the insolent smiles of the ladies, were more intolerable.

But there is more to his response than this. While listening to Mrs. Bennet, "the expression of his face changed gradually from indignant contempt to a composed and steady gravity," and during Mary's pretentious performance he refuses to share in the Bingley sisters' "derision," and instead "continued . . . impenetrably grave." Gravity is a term used in the eighteenth century to define emotions of the most serious and dignified kind. For Darcy to register such feelings thus provides clear evidence that his attitude to the Bennets is shaped not only by vanity but also by a keen sensitivity to the moral implications of their actual behaviour. Elizabeth's prejudice, however, is too strong to allow her to see what is revealed in Darcy's face, and it comes as a surprise to her when he later explains that:

> The situation of your mother's family, though objectionable, was nothing in comparison of that total want of propriety so frequently, so almost uniformly betrayed by herself, by your three younger sisters, and occasionally even by your father.

In the midst of all this confusion, discord and misunderstanding, Bingley and Jane alone achieve harmony. This is emphasised by the tableau in which the scene ends:

> They [Miss Bingley and Mrs. Hurst] repulsed every attempt of Mrs. Bennet at conversation, and by so doing, threw a languor over the whole party, which was very little relieved by the long speeches of Mr. Collins, who was complimenting Mr. Bingley and his sisters on the elegance of their entertainment, and the hospitality and politeness which had marked their behaviour to their guests. Darcy said nothing at all. Mr. Bennet, in equal silence, was enjoying the scene. Mr. Bingley and Jane were standing together, a little detached from the rest, and talked only to each other. Elizabeth preserved as steady a silence as either Mrs. Hurst or Miss Bingley.

One of the functions of the dance invitation motif has been to establish similar contrasts between Bingley's relationship with Jane and Darcy's with Elizabeth throughout the first part of the novel. While Darcy refuses to dance with Elizabeth at the Meryton Assembly, Bingley dances twice with Jane. From that point on their relationship is one of approach and acceptance in contrast to the approach and rejection pattern that characterises all meetings between Darcy and Elizabeth. Thus, at the very moment when Elizabeth is busily engaged in repudiating Darcy at the Netherfield ball, Bingley and Jane pass by "dancing together." The ease with which Bingley and Jane draw together, however, is not so much intended to offer a contrast to the difficulties which beset Darcy and Elizabeth as to make a comment on them. Darcy and Elizabeth are kept apart by the belief that a deep social rift lies between them. Bingley and Jane illustrate how mistaken they are. Although Bingley, who "inherited property to the amount of nearly an hundred thousand pounds from his father," is much wealthier than Jane, he does not regard himself as her social superior. His background is in trade, and he has not yet acquired the essential qualification of the gentleman — ownership of land. The Bennets, on the other hand, are a long-established family in possession of an estate, albeit entailed. There is, then, much to be gained on both sides from a match between a rising man of fortune and the daughter of a rather faded gentleman. Since Bingley and Jane are social equals, it is illogical that Darcy should be willing to associate with the Bingleys, but not with the Bennets. In the one case he quite properly balances off wealth and acquired gentility against low origins; in the other he perversely focuses almost entirely on the middle-class element introduced through marriage. This is perhaps because he finds it easier to accommodate himself to the faults of the Bingley family, which derive mainly from the aristocratic posturings of Caroline Bingley and Mrs. Hurst, than to the unaccustomed vulgarity of some members of the Bennet family. Elizabeth is no less perverse since, in spite of his sisters' aristocratic leanings, she accepts Bingley into her social universe, and yet she places his friend Darcy beyond the pale.

Some education is needed in order that Darcy and Elizabeth might come to recognise society as a network of interconnections broad enough to embrace Darcys, Bingleys, and Bennets, and thereby clear the way for personal reconciliation. This is provided by visits to the aristocratic worlds of Rosings and Pemberley. Life at Rosings under Lady Catherine de Bourgh confirms Elizabeth's stereotypes, but Pemberley calls them into question, and compels her to arrive at a more complex and favourable view of the aristocracy. Darcy's perspective is broadened in a similar way. The behaviour of Collins and the Lucases at Rosings displays the middle class at its worst; but the Gardiners, to whom Darcy is introduced at Pemberley, prove that trade and gentility are not incompatible. A change in the personal relationship follows almost automatically from these reversals in social attitudes, and by the end of the visit to

Pemberley Elizabeth is more than ready to accept Darcy as her suitor.

To emphasise the reversals which are achieved by the progression from Rosings to Pemberley Jane Austen organises this section of her novel around a series of antitheses. There are three main elements in Elizabeth's introduction to each house—a eulogy by a retainer, a view of the house and its park, and a meeting with the owner—and it is in the contrasts between them that the essential qualities of Rosings and Pemberley, and hence of the aristocracy, are revealed to her. The contrasting ways in which Collins and the Lucases on the one hand and the Gardiners on the other respond to aristocratic environments is equally revealing of the middle class, and provides the basis of Darcy's education. The transformation which is wrought in Darcy's relationship with Elizabeth as a result of social enlightenment is echoed in the substitution of a pattern of approach and acceptance at Pemberley for the approach and rejection motif which continues to predominate at Rosings.

Our acquaintance with Rosings begins a long time before we are actually granted a view of the estate or its owner. Mr. Collins's first letter to Mr. Bennet is full of the subject and whenever he is present thereafter, we are sure to hear more about it. Of course, none of what Collins says can be taken at face value, because it functions entirely at the level of eulogy and, in that Rosings has become his *raison d'être*, it would be hard to imagine a less objective guide. Nevertheless, he turns out to be ideal because, simply by being the kind of man he is, he captures the very spirit of the place. Indeed, it could be argued with some justice that once we know Collins we know Rosings and Lady Catherine de Bourgh. By all professional standards, Collins is completely unsuited to the clerical position granted him by Lady Catherine. Despite his displays of piety, which include subjecting the Bennet girls to readings of Fordyce, there is little evidence that he is motivated by any considerations but of self. It might be expected that a clergyman influenced by Fordyce would object to card-playing, dancing, and singing. Collins, however, does not allow such scruples to interfere with his own amusement:

> "I am by no means of opinion, I assure you," said he, "that a ball of this kind, given by a young man of character, to respectable people, can have any evil tendency; and I am so far from objecting to dancing myself that I shall hope to be honoured with the hands of all my fair cousins in the course of the evening."

Collins's outline of a clergyman's duties also places a suspiciously strong emphasis on things of advantage to himself:

> The rector of a parish has much to do. — In the first place, he must make such an agreement for tythes as may be beneficial to himself

and not offensive to his patron. He must write his own sermons; and the time that remains will not be too much for his parish duties, and the care and improvement of his dwelling, which he cannot be excused from making as comfortable as possible.

As if to compensate for laxness about his own religious obligations, Collins is excessively strenuous in dealing with the failings of others, and shows little awareness of Christian charity. The advice he offers the Bennets about Lydia's elopement, for example, runs in direct contradiction to the parable of the prodigal son: "Let me advise you then, my dear Sir, to console yourself as much as possible, to throw off your unworthy child from your affection for ever, and leave her to reap the fruits of her own heinous offence." Since Collins lacks any of the proper qualifications to be vicar of Rosings, we must assume that Lady Catherine's decision to entrust him with the spiritual life of the community under her charge was based entirely on his ability to offer her unstinted approval: "I need not say you will be delighted with her. She is all affability and condescension." This tells us something very important about how affairs are conducted at Rosings. Unlike the responsible landowner, who believes that the possession of an estate confers on him an obligation to attend to the needs of his tenants and local community, Lady Catherine, it seems, is concerned only with the ways in which Rosings can increase her own prestige. A clergyman who flatters her and broadcasts her virtue to the world is therefore preferable to one who takes his profession seriously.

Mrs. Reynolds, Darcy's housekeeper, who introduces Elizabeth and the Gardiners to Pemberley, offers an equally illuminating but contrasting insight into the operations of the aristocratic estate. The manner in which she praises her employer has something of the eulogy about it too, and, in answering Mr. Gardiner's comment about the possibility of Darcy marrying, she undoubtedly exaggerates his virtues: "Yes, Sir; but I do not know when *that* will be. I do not know who is good enough for him." However, whereas sycophantic regard for rank inspires Collins's hyperboles about Lady Catherine, it is the genuine "pride" and "attachment" of an "intelligent servant" that cause Mrs. Reynolds to speak so well of Darcy. Her knowledge of Darcy, his family, and his house is intimate. She can speak with authority not only about Darcy's excellent conduct as master of Pemberley, but also of his virtues as a four-year-old child; she was personally acquainted with old Mr. Darcy and, through their portraits, knows of the family forbears; and she can give precise information about the functions and trappings of every room in the Pemberley house. The master-servant relationship thus revealed is the proper one. Darcy does not expect his employees to be grovelling subordinates, but regards them as sensible human beings whose respect must be earned. Neither does he see them simply as instruments of labour, but rather as rational human beings who must be included in the community of the big house and introduced to Pemberley values in order that they might play their part in preserving proper social standards.

The second element in Elizabeth's introduction to the aristocratic world is her first view of the two great houses. A distant prospect of Rosings suggests that it was built to sustain a worthwhile ideal: "It was a handsome modern building, well situated on rising ground." However, as interpreted by Mr. Collins, whose tone is rapturous, and whose attention is fixed on the number and cost of the windows, it comes to represent pretension and materialism:

> Every park has its beauty and its prospects; and Elizabeth saw much to be pleased with, though she could not be in such raptures as Mr. Collins expected the scene to inspire, and was but slightly affected by his enumeration of the windows in front of the house, and his relations of what the glazing altogether had originally cost Sir Lewis De Bourgh.

The interior reveals a similar discrepancy between original intention and present function. The entrance hall is of "fine proportion," but the furniture substitutes "splendour" for "elegance."

Pemberley is not marred by any such failed ideals. At first sight the park and the house not only create an impression of great dignity but also display that balance of Art and Nature which in the eighteenth century indicated moral worth as well as aesthetic value.

> It was a large, handsome, stone building, standing well on rising ground, and backed by a ridge of high woody hills; — and in front, a stream of some natural importance was swelled into greater, but without any artificial appearance. Its banks were neither formal, nor falsely adorned. Elizabeth was delighted. She had never seen a place for which nature had done more, or where natural beauty had been so little counteracted by an awkward taste.

Even when viewed from different perspectives through the windows of the house, the grounds retain their perfection: "As they passed into other rooms, these objects were taking different positions; but from every window there were beauties to be seen." The interior of Pemberley, with its lofty and handsome rooms, and furniture which is "neither gaudy nor uselessly fine," contributes further to the sense of proper proportion, dignity, and taste.

Given the contrasts between retainers and estates, it is hardly surprising that the owners of Rosings and Pemberley, to whom Elizabeth is next introduced, should be very different. Lady Catherine de Bourgh, as Elizabeth anticipates, possesses neither "extraordinary talents [n]or miraculous virtue" and depends for her prestige on "the mere stateliness of money and rank." As hostess, it is her duty to set her guests at their ease. However, far from acknowledging this obligation, she treats them in a manner designed to make them fully aware of their inferior rank, and obviously expects the kind of sycophantic response she receives from Mr. Collins and Sir William Lucas at dinner:

> He carved, and ate, and praised with delighted alacrity; and every dish was commended, first by him, and then by Sir William, who was now enough recovered to echo whatever his son-in-law said, in a manner which Elizabeth wondered Lady Catherine could bear. But Lady Catherine seemed gratified by their excessive admiration, and gave most gracious smiles.

A sense of superiority also characterises Lady Catherine's conversational mode. The guests are relieved of any responsibility to initiate or even to participate in conversation. Their task is simply to listen and be informed as Lady Catherine pronounces authoritatively on a variety of subjects:

> When the ladies returned to the drawing room, there was little to be done but to hear Lady Catherine talk, which she did without any intermission till coffee came in, delivering her opinion on every subject in so decisive a manner as proved that she was not used to have her judgment controverted.

The god-like role she assumes here is even more evident at the end of the evening when "the party . . . gathered round the fire to hear Lady Catherine determine what weather they were to have on the morrow."

Further acquaintance soon reveals to Elizabeth that a similar sense of absolute authority characterises Lady Catherine's behaviour even beyond the confines of her own house. During visits to the Hunsford parsonage she presumes to comment on all aspects of Mrs. Collins's housekeeping, and she uses her traditional position as leader of the local community as an excuse for interfering in the lives of the villagers:

> Elizabeth soon perceived that though this great lady was not in the commission of the peace for the county, she was a most active magistrate in her own parish, the minutest concerns of which were carried to her by Mr. Collins; and whenever any of the cottagers were disposed to be quarrelsome, discontented, or too poor, she sallied forth into the village to settle their differences, silence their complaints, and scold them into harmony and plenty.

Neo-feudal arrogance, however, is not the mark of all aristocrats, and Darcy greets his guests, uninvited though they are, in a very different style. Even though he is embarrassed to meet Elizabeth, Darcy nevertheless makes "civil inquiries after her family," and conducts himself with extreme modesty: "Never in her life had she seen his manners so little dignified, never had he spoken with such gentleness." As an acknowledgment of Elizabeth's worth, Darcy expresses a wish to introduce her to his sister, thereby paying her "a compliment of the highest kind." "Civility" also characterises Darcy's reaction to the Gardiners, even after he learns that they are in trade. Such good manners suggest that the needs of his guests, rather than his own importance, are uppermost in Darcy's mind, and he performs two acts that confirm this impression. When Mr. Gardiner expresses an interest in angling, Darcy immediately invites him to fish at Pemberley; and when he observes that Mrs. Gardiner is tired, he presses her to take refreshments in his house. In their review of Darcy's behaviour, the Gardiners declare him to be "perfectly well behaved, polite, and unassuming" and "really attentive."

Darcy is given a similar lesson in middle-class *mores* by the contrast between the manners of Collins and Sir William Lucas at Rosings, and the Gardiners at Pemberley. For a man such as Darcy, whose sense of human dignity is keenly developed, the clownish grovelling of Mr. Collins and Sir William Lucas is perhaps even more offensive than the aggressive rudeness of Mrs. Bennet. In any case, it cannot help but confirm his conviction that middle-class behaviour fails to serve the proper ends of polite intercourse. Far from contributing to an atmosphere of harmony and mutual respect, Collins and Sir William, as we have already seen, succeed only in encouraging Lady Catherine to indulge in further displays of overweening vanity.

The Gardiners' acquaintance with the aristocracy can hardly be more extensive than Sir William Lucas's. But they realise that there are certain absolute standards of politeness, and are thus able to greet Darcy with a proper mixture of dignity and respect: "She listened most attentively to all that passed between them, and gloried in every expression, every sentence of her uncle, which marked his intelligence, his taste, or his good manners." Mr. Gardiner does not demean himself by expressing awe at the grandeur of his companion, but rather turns the conversation to fishing, a topic he can anticipate will be of mutual interest to himself and to the owner of well-stocked streams. At the same time, the Gardiners do not let the notice of a great gentleman go to their heads. Whereas Collins grasps at every crumb of attention Lady Catherine lets fall his way, they are careful to ensure that a proper distance is maintained. Therefore, when Darcy invites them to enter his house, they politely refuse.

The two visits, then, contribute greatly to the social education of Elizabeth and Darcy. Elizabeth learns that while a sense of their own importance does make some aristocrats unpleasantly condescending in their relationships with their "inferiors" and neglectful of their social obligations, nevertheless this is not true of the group as a whole. Life at Pemberley is characterised by a concern for others and an attention to duty which operate on such a grand scale that Elizabeth at last becomes aware that the aristocrat has good reason to be proud. The limitations of Darcy's stereotypes are exposed with equal thoroughness. The middle class is more than Mr. Collins and Sir William Lucas, and to label it as improper and vulgar is to do an injustice to people like the Gardiners, who not only know their duty but can perform it like "people of fashion."

This social enlightenment has profound consequences for Darcy and Elizabeth's relationship, and these can be best demonstrated by examining the contrasting patterns of interaction that characterise their encounters at Rosings and Pemberley. Elizabeth's poor opinion of the aristocracy is confirmed by acquaintance with Lady Catherine and by the revelation that Darcy effected the separation between Bingley and Jane: "[Darcy's] pride, she was convinced, would receive a deeper wound from the want of importance in his friend's connections, than from their want of sense; and she was quite decided at last, that he had been partly governed by this worst kind of pride." Similarly, further contact with the middle class does not make Darcy any more ready to admit that Elizabeth's virtues owe anything to her background: "*You* cannot have a right to such very strong local attachment. *You* cannot have been always at Longbourn." Consequently, their meetings at Rosings continue to follow a pattern of approach and rejection.

Darcy quite literally draws near to Elizabeth during an evening at Rosings, but she is unwilling to acknowledge his claims to attention, and greets him with an arch and hostile comment:

> You mean to frighten me, Mr. Darcy, by coming in all this state to hear me? But I will not be alarmed though your sister *does* play so well. There is stubbornness about me that never can bear to be frightened at the will of others. My courage always rises with every attempt to intimidate me.

Darcy, however, fails to heed the clear hint that Elizabeth still regards him as a snob, and continues in his efforts to engage her in conversation. Elizabeth consequently becomes more directly aggressive, and tries to embarrass Darcy by resurrecting her old grievance about his refusal to dance at the Meryton ball. Darcy sidesteps the implicit, and quite accurate, charge that he behaved snobbishly on that occasion, and pleads diffidence and shyness in conversation with new people; but Elizabeth refuses to be placated. Skilfully changing the point of attack, she argues that it is his duty to develop social graces:

> "I certainly have not the talent which some people possess," said
> Darcy, "of conversing easily with those I have never seen
> before . . ."
> "My fingers," said Elizabeth, "do not move over this instrument
> in the masterly manner which I see so many women's do . . . But
> then I have always supposed it to be my own fault—because I would
> not take the trouble of practising."

Her advice is good, but her aim is to rebuff Darcy's present advance rather than
to improve his future conduct.

Darcy's subsequent approaches are no more successful. Elizabeth receives his
first visit to the parsonage politely enough, but by refusing to believe that it was
inspired by anything more than boredom, she deprives his overture of friendship
of its significance. Further visits in company with Colonel Fitzwilliam merely
convince Elizabeth that Darcy is inferior to his cousin. While he continues to
place himself in her presence whenever possible, failure to establish communication with someone he now loves deeply increasingly incapacitates Darcy:

> More than once did Elizabeth in her ramble within the Park, unex-
> pectedly meet Mr. Darcy.—She felt all the perverseness of the mis-
> chance that should bring him where no one else was brought; and to
> prevent its ever happening again, took care to inform him at first,
> that it was a favourite haunt of hers.—How it could occur a second
> time therefore was very odd!—Yet it did, and even a third. It seemed
> like wilful ill-nature, or a voluntary penance, for on these occasions it
> was not merely a few formal enquiries and an awkward pause and
> then away, but he actually thought it necessary to turn back and
> walk with her. He never said a great deal, nor did she give herself the
> trouble of talking or of listening much.

Thus, no foundation of mutual understanding has been laid before Darcy
makes the ultimate gesture of communication by asking Elizabeth to marry him.
His hopes of success are based on recognition of a certain receptiveness to his approaches. However, Elizabeth is not conscious of any feelings other than dislike
and, since his proposal is phrased in a condescending and almost unwilling way
that proves he has not overcome his original prejudices, she once again rejects
him. The only difference is that now she makes her objections explicit:

> From the very beginning, from the first moment I may almost say, of
> my acquaintance with you, your manners impressing me with the
> fullest belief of your arrogance, your conceit, and your selfish disdain

of the feelings of others, were such as to form that ground-work of disapprobation, on which succeeding events have built so immove-able a dislike; and I had not known you a month before I felt that you were the last man in the world whom I could ever be prevailed on to marry.

The tone of finality here is even greater than when Elizabeth and Darcy parted at the Netherfield ball. Yet, in their next series of meetings at Pemberley, a pattern of approach and acceptance prevails. The seed of this change is contained, paradoxically, within what seems to be the most complete of all rejections. Elizabeth's rebuke and Darcy's subsequent explanation force each to give fresh consideration to the validity of his prejudices. Reassessment is rapidly completed by exposure to the best of each other's worlds at Pemberley, and Elizabeth is at last able to acknowledge her feelings for Darcy.

Emotional liberation begins with Elizabeth's first view of Pemberley: "at that moment she felt, that to be mistress of Pemberley might be something!" And it is completed by the realisation that Darcy will accept her uncle and aunt, whom she had believed would be lost to her if she married him. Darcy's approaches at last meet with success. Elizabeth agrees to receive his sister, then to dine at Pemberley, and finally she makes a spontaneous approach to Darcy by returning Georgiana's visit. Whereas emotional immaturity blinded Elizabeth to the significance of Darcy's earlier ritual manoeuvrings, she is now fully aware of the significance of his approaches and of her own response:

> He who, she had been persuaded, would avoid her as his greatest enemy, seemed, on this accidental meeting, most eager to preserve the acquaintance, and without any indelicate display of regard, or any peculiarity of manner, where their two selves only were concerned, was soliciting the good opinion of her friends, and bent on making her known to his sister. Such a change in a man of so much pride, excited not only astonishment but gratitude—for to love, ardent love, it must be attributed; and as such its impression on her was of a sort to be encouraged, as by no means unpleasing, though it could not be exactly defined. She respected, she esteemed, she was grateful to him, she felt a real interest in his welfare.

After the morning visit to Pemberley, Darcy makes a public declaration of his admiration for Elizabeth: "it is many months since I have considered her as one of the handsomest women of my acquaintance." Marriage now seems close, but before Elizabeth can fulfill her dinner engagement she is called away from Pemberley by the news of Lydia's elopement. Jane Austen delays her main action in this way so that Darcy's acceptance of the Bennets might be fully tested. He must endure three trials, each of which ends in a marriage, the third being his own. The first, and most difficult, arises directly out of the elopement. Since mere impropriety had been enough to evoke Darcy's scorn earlier, the gross immorality of Lydia's actions clearly puts an intense strain on his revised opinion of the middle class. However, helped by the feeling that he is partly to blame himself, for keeping his knowledge of Wickham's previous misdemeanours secret, Darcy is able to avoid drawing general social conclusions from Lydia's behaviour. Thus, far from rejecting the Bennet family, he demonstrates an active concern with their affairs by becoming involved in the search for Lydia and Wickham, and by helping to arrange their marriage.

Although not as severe as the first, the other two tests are nevertheless trying for a man as proud as Darcy. Recognition that he has been wrong to reject the Bennet family in its entirety because of the failings of some of its members involves Darcy in the humiliating task of telling Bingley that he should not have persuaded him to separate from Jane. His reward, however, is Bingley and Jane's rapid renewal of affection and engagement to marry. Finally, Darcy must atone for his mistreatment of Mrs. Bennet. This he does during a dinner at Longbourn. Mrs. Bennet does not make things easy for Darcy. Under her tutelage, the party is conducted with that lack of regard for conversational opportunities that Darcy hates, especially as it means he has almost no chance to talk to Elizabeth:

> The gentlemen came; and she thought he looked as if he would have answered her hopes; but alas! the ladies had crowded round the table, where Miss Bennet was making tea, and Elizabeth pouring out the coffee, in so close a confederacy, that there was not a single vacancy near her, which would admit of a chair . . . When the tea-things were removed, and the card tables placed, the ladies all rose, and Elizabeth was then hoping to be soon joined by him, when all her views were overthrown, by seeing him fall a victim to her mother's rapacity for whist players.

Furthermore, Mrs. Bennet makes no attempt to conceal her long-standing resentment of Darcy, and when she sits next to him she is ungracious. In such circumstances, Darcy does well simply to avoid rudeness, but in fact, as Mrs. Bennet admits, he even manages to pay her a few conventional compliments: "The soup was fifty times better than what we had at the Lucas's last week; and even Mr. Darcy acknowledged, that the partridges were remarkably well done." Darcy's forbearance is rewarded with yet another marriage. A few days later he renews his proposal, and is accepted by Elizabeth. Thus by the time the sequence of marriages has been completed, all conflicts and misunderstandings have been resolved, and Darcy and Elizabeth have been placed firmly at the centre of a world characterised by a sense of order and harmony.

This union of aristocracy and gentry-middle class is not achieved easily; but it is possible, Jane Austen claims, because, despite their different social roles, the two groups are united by a shared ideal of concern for others. As Elizabeth tells Lady Catherine: "In marrying your nephew, I should not consider myself as quitting that sphere. He is a gentleman; I am a gentleman's daughter; so far we are equal." The moral strength of Pemberley, then, is not based so much on the exclusion of disruptive forces, although Lydia and Wickham are banned, but on the inclusion of responsible people from the aristocracy, the gentry, and the middle class. Darcy and Elizabeth are resident, Bingley and Jane live close by, and the Gardiners from Gracechurch Street are the most welcome of visitors: "With the Gardiners, they were always on the most intimate terms. Darcy, as well as Elizabeth, really loved them."

This vision of order and harmony is not expressed thematically until marriage resolves Elizabeth and Darcy's conflicts. However, it is implicit throughout in the novel's highly-patterned structure, based on the dance invitation motif, the visits to Rosings and Pemberley, the final sequence of marriages, and an overall pattern of approach-rejection-acceptance. Form and content are truly one in *Pride and Prejudice.*

Intelligence
in *Pride and Prejudice*

Susan Morgan

Pride and Prejudice has a charmed place as the most popular of Austen's novels. Elizabeth, witty, self-confident, with those dancing eyes, and not quite beautiful face, depicts for all of us what is flawed and irresistible about real people. Trilling has observed about *Emma* that we like Mr. Knightley "because we perceive that he cherishes Emma not merely in spite of her subversive self-assertion but because of it." This applies to Mr. Darcy as well, and Elizabeth, perfectly aware that it does, cannot resist inquiring when she demands an account of his having fallen in love with her: "Did you admire me for my impertinence?" Her impertinence, of course, is why generations of readers have admired her and why we recognize that the major concern of the book is with the possibilities and responsibility of free and lively thought. *Pride and Prejudice* explores the special question of the meaning of freedom, given the premise which Austen assumes throughout her fiction, that the relation between character and public reality is at once difficult and necessary.

Elizabeth's freedom is basically the freedom to think for herself. Unlike Catherine Morland and Emma Woodhouse, one of whom follows external structures and the other of whom is preoccupied with creating her own, Elizabeth sees herself as already beyond those forms which direct or control our perceptions. She begins her story believing that she does judge from her own observations rather than from preconceptions. But like Catherine and Emma, Elizabeth is self-deceived. We watch her move from a belief in her own logic to a more fluid interpretation of knowing and of intelligence in terms of the backgrounds, contexts, and particulars which inform truth. And we learn to

From *In the Meantime: Character and Perception in Jane Austen's Fiction.* © 1980 by The University of Chicago. The University of Chicago Press, 1980.

acknowledge that the pressing importance of such a movement rests not on our hopes for being right but on our hopes for being free.

Miss Bingley describes Elizabeth's free spirit as "an abominable sort of conceited independence, a most country town indifference to decorum." Certainly, Elizabeth hurrying through the muddy countryside to visit Jane, springing over puddles and jumping over stiles, is not a decorous sight. And just as certainly, those muddy petticoats and glowing cheeks contribute a great deal to Mr. Darcy's falling in love. The importance of Elizabeth's sense of freedom and the necessity of relating that idea to her growth in the novel may account for the fact that so many critics have sought to discuss *Pride and Prejudice* in terms of a dualism (suggested by the title) in which Elizabeth's freedom constitutes one pole and some sort of social sense the other. Her progress can then be understood as a movement from polarity to a merging or harmony, represented by her marriage to Mr. Darcy. Thus Alistair Duckworth finds it generally agreed that *Pride and Prejudice* "achieves an ideal relation between the individual and society." Dorothy Van Ghent sees the book as illuminating "the difficult and delicate reconciliation of the sensitively developed individual with the terms of his social existence." Marvin Mudrick, then, would account for Elizabeth's wrong-headedness as a failure to acknowledge the social context, and Samuel Kliger, in variant terms, places the dichotomy as that between nature and art. All would locate the embodiment of that final harmony among the stately and tasteful grounds of Pemberley.

Although most of these individual discussions, and others like them, are both valuable and persuasive, they share that familiar assumption which in Austen criticism has sunk to a truism, that her perspective is one of social and rational good. The general objection to this prevailing view is its orderliness when applied to *Pride and Prejudice*. It is hard to see where in that vision of social and emotional harmony with which so many would have the novel end there could be room for the doubts, the blindness, and the mistakes which Elizabeth still exhibits and which are a continuing part of every major character Austen creates. I do not at all mean to imply that beyond the lightness there is some dark side to the novelist, some sort of regulated hatred or repression. I do mean to ask where there would be room for the life which, as Austen was perfectly aware, goes on beyond all our formulations of it. [Stuart M.] Tave reminds us that "She knows, and she shows in her novels, messy lives, and most people are leading them, even when the surface of life seems proper." We have been too eager to assume that Austen's was a conclusive vision, a sort of apotheosis of the optimism of premodern fiction. To understand *Pride and Prejudice* in terms of some ideal blend of the individual and the social is to speak of finalities about a writer who herself chooses to speak of the possible, the continuous, the incomplete. Austen's "social" concerns are with human relations, not society. Her own reference to "the little bit (two inches wide) of Ivory" can only be called unfortunate in the light of the critical weight given that suspiciously humble remark. Austen offers neither Chinese miniatures nor Dutch interiors nor any surface so finished that meanings are conclusive as well. It is hardly possible to speak of her themes as social (or as rational) without involving, by implication alone, that too familiar image of her as outside her own time and belonging to an earlier and more ordered age.

A more particular objection to the prevailing view of *Pride and Prejudice* is that it violates the evidence of the text. If Mr. Darcy is to represent society and Elizabeth a rebellious individualism, how can we account for the fact that the first major breach of society's rules is made by Mr. Darcy, when he insults Elizabeth within her hearing at the Meryton ball? It seems evasive to conclude, with Mary Lascelles, that at the moment Mr. Darcy is out of character and the remark is a technical flaw. Unquestionably, Mr. Darcy is an outstanding member of society, a landowner with both power and responsibility. His position and an accompanying sense of duties and obligations justify a proper kind of pride. Yet this should not obscure the fact that Mr. Darcy's nature, far from being social, is reserved, independent, isolated, private, and vain. And it is Elizabeth who points to this discrepancy when she remarks to Colonel Fitzwilliam on Mr. Darcy's rude conduct at the Meryton dance: "Shall we ask him why a man of sense and education, and who has lived in the world, is ill qualified to recommend himself to strangers?"

Elizabeth's failures in judgment, with Charlotte Lucas but primarily with Mr. Wickham and Mr. Darcy, cannot be adequately explained as a headstrong insistence on private judgment in the face of social values. It is inaccurate to claim that Elizabeth should have been swayed by the fact that Mr. Wickham "is a dispossessed man in an acquisitive society" (Marvin Mudrick). He has a military commission, and military service, like naval service, is an honorable, gentlemanly occupation composing a respected part of Austen's social scheme. It would be just as distorting for Elizabeth to find Mr. Darcy socially acceptable simply because he owns Pemberley, whatever Charlotte Lucas may think. It is Charlotte, after all, who advises Elizabeth "not to be a simpleton and allow her fancy for Wickham to make her appear unpleasant in the eyes of a man of ten times his consequence." Charlotte chooses "not to be a simpleton" and will spend the rest of her life with Mr. Collins. To judge others in economic or social terms is the very sort of thinking Austen would expose. Mr. Wickham is socially unacceptable for moral rather than economic reasons—not because he has no possessions but because he has no principles. Judging him is no more a question of manners than it is of position or money. Mr. Wickham can be as pleasantly talkative and polite as Mr. Darcy can be unpleasantly reserved and rude. Elizabeth misjudges them both, but not through an individualism that fails to appreciate class or social values. If that were true, *Pride and Prejudice* would be a lesser novel. Elizabeth's failure is one of intelligence.

Austen's major study of the links between intelligence and freedom is cast as a love story, one which she delighted in describing as "rather too light, and bright and sparkling." Most of the action of *Pride and Prejudice* can be accounted for as a tale of love which violates the traditions of romance. The rather unromantic beginnings of Henry Tilney's affection for Catherine Morland have been expanded into a prominent motif about the lovers in *Pride and Prejudice*. For much of the story, Mr. Darcy cares for Elizabeth in spite of herself, and she does not care for him at all. When Elizabeth comes to have feelings for Mr. Darcy she understands her change as above all "a motive within her of good will which could not be overlooked. It was gratitude. — Gratitude, not merely for having once loved her, but for loving her still well enough, to forgive all the petulance and acrimony of her manner in rejecting him, and all the unjust accusations accompanying her rejection." Such a motive for love may not be ideal, but it has the author's full approval. It is also shared by Jane Bennet, the character in *Pride and Prejudice* who comes closest to providing standards of true sensibility. Jane explains to Elizabeth her own goodwill to Mr. Darcy on the grounds that "I always had a value for him. Were it for nothing but his love of you, I must always have esteemed him."

The emotional appeal of someone being in love with you is a favorite theme of Austen's. It draws Marianne Dashwood to Colonel Brandon as well as Henry Tilney to Catherine and even, in a more comical way, Harriet Smith to the long-suffering farmer Martin. It may help to explain Jane Fairfax's love for Frank Churchill, and it is strong enough to begin to lure Fanny Price toward Henry Crawford and finally to win Edmund Bertram for her. Its most powerful expression is in *Persuasion*, in the intense and muted feelings of Anne Elliot and Captain Wentworth. There love reawakens love in an almost Shelleyan cycle of reciprocity. The particular significance of this theme in *Pride and Prejudice* is that Elizabeth's gratitude and increasing affection for Mr. Darcy are inseparable from her intellectual growth. Right and wrong thinking in the novel can be measured in terms of Elizabeth's changing feelings toward Mr. Darcy and Mr. Wickham. Against Mr. Wickham's empty charm Elizabeth must balance the dangers and obligations of a demanding love. Gratitude, then, is the response by means of which Austen seeks to define freedom and intelligence within the binding circumstances of emotions, partial understandings, and incomplete truths.

The progress in *Pride and Prejudice* should not then be described as a polarity resolved. Elizabeth's mistakes are not based on a rejection of society even though it is quite true that they are related to her sense of personal freedom. What we are to understand by that freedom is not the right to do and say whatever she wants in defiance of social conventions. Rather, it is a freedom to keep from becoming involved. This is why Elizabeth's education is most appropriately a love story. Trilling has said that *Pride and Prejudice* shows us that morality can be a matter of style. It also shows us that intelligence can be a matter of the heart. Elizabeth believes that understanding, intelligence, and perception depend on being independent of their objects, and she wants most powerfully to be an intelligent observer of her world. That urge explains much of her continuing appeal and is the single most important force in her story. But for Elizabeth it also means to stand apart from events. Her lesson is the particularly harsh one her father has imparted: people are blind and silly, and only distance can save her from being blind and silly as well. The view from that distance is necessarily ironic. For Elizabeth, then, being disengaged seems the only salvation from stupidity.

Elizabeth's heart is not engaged by Mr. Wickham, her understanding is. Her opinion of him is based on her belief in her own discernment and her separation through intelligence from an essentially ugly world. Elizabeth's weapon against what she sees as stupidity and ugliness is her laughter, her impertinence, and her uncommitted heart. Andrew Wright has argued with some power that "against clarity, in *Pride and Prejudice*, involvement is set." Yet his position is so unfortunately similar to Mr. Bennet's that it needs modification. Mr. Bennet's clarity offers the protection against the pains of misjudgment and disillusion which only a disinterested cynicism can provide. Involvement, it is true, can give no such protection. Yet the point of Elizabeth's story is surely that she is always involved, and her recognition of that fact brings her the kind of openness which in turn makes clarity possible.

In defending Elizabeth's affection for Mr. Darcy in language almost identical with that she had used in defending Henry Tilney's for Catherine, Austen makes the alternative quite explicit:

> If gratitude and esteem are good foundations of affection, Elizabeth's change of sentiment will be neither improbable nor faulty. But if otherwise, if the regard springing from such sources is unreasonable or unnatural, in comparison of what is so often described as arising on a first interview with its object, and even before two words have been exchanged, nothing can be said in her defence, except that she had given somewhat of a trial to the latter method, in her partiality for Wickham, and that its ill-success might perhaps authorize her to seek the other less interesting mode of attachment.

The love at first sight that Elizabeth had tried with Mr. Wickham was curiously cold, much as the flirtation between Frank Churchill and Emma was cold. This is clear when Wickham becomes "the admirer of some one else. Elizabeth was watchful enough to see it all, but she could see it and write of it without material pain. Her heart had been but slightly touched, and her vanity was satisfied with believing that *she* would have been his only choice, had fortune permitted it." Elizabeth's attraction for Mr. Wickham cannot be accounted for as a misplaced affection. The discrepancy between how Austen presents Mr. Wickham and how Elizabeth sees him leads us to understand the falseness of Elizabeth's vision.

There is a similarity of temperament (if not character) between Elizabeth and Mr. Wickham, much as there is between Emma and Frank Churchill. What these characters share is a great deal of charm, a charm that comes from a liveliness of mind as interested in what is entertaining as in what is good and right. Mr. Wickham's villainy must limit the comparison. Frank Churchill is merely irresponsible; his principles are sound. Yet Mr. Wickham's black character should not be understood as a cruder and more extreme version of Frank's, in spite of Austen's general commitment to mixed character as superior both in terms of realism and technique. The first comment on Mr. Wickham that Austen provides us with, when that interesting stranger has appeared on the street in Meryton with Mr. Denny, and the Bennet sisters are being informed that he has accepted a commission in the corps, is that "this was exactly as it should be; for the young man wanted only regimentals to make him completely charming." One wonders immediately what sort of charm would best present itself in the scarlet uniform of the militia. And Austen goes on to say that his "appearance was greatly in his favour; he had all the best part of beauty, a fine countenance, a good figure, and very pleasing address. The introduction was followed up on his side by a happy readiness of conversation—a readiness at the same time perfectly correct and unassuming." This description, unlike Austen's usual introductions in the novel, tells us nothing of Mr. Wickham's qualities or nature, but only of his looks and manners. His looks and manners are all that Elizabeth has noticed. And it will turn out that they are all Mr. Wickham has to recommend him.

Mr. Wickham, as the villain that Frank Churchill could never be, is a familiar type. That Austen meant the reader to be aware of Wickham's conventionality is established in many scenes. A late example is Jane Bennet's horrified reaction to the discovery that Mr. Wickham is "a gamester!" There is no need to explain this response, as Henrietta Ten Harmsel does, as a bit of moralizing creeping into an otherwise sophisticated structure. The point Austen wants is not that for Jane Bennet (or her author) gambling is as bad or worse than eloping with Lydia, but that Wickham's gambling fixes his character and so leaves no doubt how the elopement is to be understood. After this Jane says no more of her hope that Wickham's intentions are honorable. She knows the kind of man he is and so must we. Wickham is something of a cliché, both in his false face as a charming young man and in his true face as a fortune hunter. This lack of originality in Wickham's portrait can have nothing to do with any lack of skill on the author's part. We need only think of Mr. Collins, who belongs in the tradition of pious Christian hypocrites but whose character has so many peculiarities that he stands unabashedly on his own. We must then ask why Austen, with her explicit contempt for the stock villain, would place such a character in *Pride and Prejudice*.

Mr. Wickham is most appropriately dressed in the uniform of the militia because he is a type rather than an individual. He is one of a class of men whom Lydia and Kitty, like their mother before them, are wild about. Mr. Wickham, to be sure, is a particularly good-looking version, and this distinction is not unnoticed by another of the Bennet sisters during that first dinner: "When Mr. Wickham walked into the room, Elizabeth felt that she had neither been seeing him before, nor thinking of him since, with the smallest degree of unreasonable admiration. The officers of the ——shire were in general a very creditable, gentlemanlike set, and the best of them were of the present party; but Mr. Wickham was as far beyond them all in person, countenance, air, and walk, as *they* were superior to the broad-faced stuffy uncle Philips." We cannot but notice how commonplace and how coldly evaluative this response is from the girl whose judgment is supposed to be special. Near the end of *Northanger Abbey* Austen, in her role as conventional novelist, reassures us that Eleanor Tilney's new husband, though he has not actually appeared in the story, is "to a precision the most charming young man in the world." She goes on to observe, "Any further definition of his merits must be unnecessary; the most charming young man in the world is instantly before the imagination of us all."

This idea, with its overtones of literary convention, is used more critically in *Pride and Prejudice*. How closely Mr. Wickham qualifies as Elizabeth's ideal of the most charming young man in the world may be guessed from her conviction, after taking leave for Hunsford, that "he must always be her model of the amiable and pleasing." The airy fictional tone of their relations, so like that between Henry Crawford and the Bertram sisters, is established from the beginning in the account of their first conversation: "Mr. Wickham was the happy man towards whom almost every female eye was turned, and Elizabeth was the happy woman by whom he finally seated himself; and the agreeable manner in which he immediately fell into conversation, though it was only on its being a wet night, and on the probability of a rainy season, made her feel that the commonest, dullest, and most threadbare topic might be rendered interesting by the skill of the speaker." The feelings and behavior of the "happy" pair are obvious clichés, an

effect delightfully reinforced by Austen's reference to Mr. Wickham and the
other officers as Mr. Collins's "rivals for the notice of the fair." We notice
Elizabeth's self-deception, her lack of any serious feelings for this handsome
young officer about whom, as she is to realize later, she knows nothing at all.

Mr. Wickham's kind of charm, one of public and superficial ease, makes
him seem unreal. He is a flat character moving amongst actual people. This is
achieved in part through the fact that Austen has Wickham himself make up his
public role. The aesthetic and the moral responsibility for creating a typical rake
must lie with Wickham rather than with his author. It is an excellent method,
for Wickham, though villainous, is neither subtle nor ingenious, and the mask
he creates for Meryton's benefit and his own is tellingly unoriginal. One need only notice the silliness of the sad tale he recites to Elizabeth, in its style as well as its
sentiments:

> "It is not for *me* to be driven away by Mr. Darcy. If *he* wishes to
> avoid seeing *me*, he must go. . . . His father, Miss Bennet, the late
> Mr. Darcy, was one of the best men that ever breathed, and the
> truest friend I ever had; and I can never be in company with this Mr.
> Darcy without being grieved to the soul by a thousand tender
> recollections. His behaviour to myself has been scandalous; but I
> verily believe I could forgive him any thing and every thing, rather
> than his disappointing the hopes and disgracing the memory of his
> father."

He is as trite a scoundrel as he has been a pretended hero. His unsettled life, his indifference to Lydia, his debts and applications for money through her, are all bor-
ingly predictable. We are taught by the very language of the book, by the style of
Wickham's life and conversations and the style of his author's descriptions, that
he is not to be taken seriously, that he is just a made-up character, only a fiction
after all. But for the characters in *Pride and Prejudice* Wickham is not some conventional villain in a novel. And, of course, his villainy has real consequences.
Certainly in life there are people who are stereotypes, those limited to the super-
ficiality and the insidious simplicity of living in roles. Like Willoughby in *Sense
and Sensibility*, Wickham lacks the moral imagination to develop and so defines
the limits rather than the possibilities of character.

Wickham is a danger to the very innocent (Georgiana Darcy) and the very
wild (Lydia Bennet). Even Mr. Darcy acknowledges at the Netherfield ball that
"Mr. Wickham is blessed with such happy manners as may ensure his *making*
friends — whether he may be equally capable of *retaining* them, is less certain."
Mr. Wickham does succeed in being universally liked in Meryton. Yet we must
ask why Elizabeth, who is neither innocent nor wild nor like everyone else in

Meryton, is also completely taken in. The first we know of Elizabeth is Mr. Bennet's laconic observation that "they are all silly and ignorant like other girls; but Lizzy has something more of quickness than her sisters." Yet to be praised by Mr. Bennet is a questionable recommendation, since by quickness he must surely mean the discernment of other people's follies. This is the way Mr. Bennet has chosen to exercise his own faculties and the way he has taught his daughter, by example and encouragement, to apply hers. Elizabeth is quick to see and laugh at the failings of many — of the Bingley sisters, of Mr. Collins, of Mr. Bingley, of her own family, and even of Jane. Yet she chooses not to see Mr. Wickham, and this in spite of the fact that she is provided with obvious evidence of his falseness — in his absurdly sentimental choices of expressions, in the discrepancies between his assertions and his behavior, and in the very improbability of his story.

Elizabeth can be charmed by Wickham and can accept his story precisely because he and his story are such clichés. Elizabeth's self-deception does not lie, like Emma's, in being a creator of one's own interesting fictions. Nor does it, like Catherine Morland's, consist of playing a created character, except for that touch at the end of the novel when she and Mr. Darcy discuss whether the moral of their story will come out as it should. If Emma behaves like an author and Catherine like a character, then Elizabeth behaves like a reader. Another way to say this is simply that Elizabeth neither manipulates people nor acts like a heroine herself. Instead, she understands herself as an observer, an enlightened and discerning witness to all that is ridiculous and entertaining in others. Austen is again concerned with a character's response to novelistic conventions. But in Elizabeth's case the problem lies in using stories as a means of disengaging oneself from experience. Elizabeth frequently places herself in the presumably disinterested position of someone watching yet apart. In the drawing room at Netherfield "Elizabeth was so much caught by what passed, as to leave her very little attention for her book; and soon laying it wholly aside, she drew near the card-table." The next evening "Elizabeth took up some needlework, and was sufficiently amused in attending to what passed between Darcy and his companion." She takes up much the same positions at Hunsford and even within her own home. In Elizabeth's attitude we see the influence of Mr. Bennet's cynical credo that "For what do we live, but to make sport for our neighbours, and to laugh at them in our turn?"

Elizabeth's observations are far from being as irresponsible and limiting as her father's. She tells Mr. Darcy that "I hope I never ridicule what is wise or good. Follies and nonsense, whims and inconsistencies *do* divert me, I own, and I laugh at them whenever I can." Elizabeth can do more than laugh. She is able to credit Charlotte's sensible domestic arrangements as much as she delights in the absurdities of Mr. Collins. She can sympathize with Jane's suffering and can condemn the impropriety and the evil of her father's misused intelligence. Indeed, the variety of Elizabeth's observations and the degree to which she enjoys them are basic to her charm. Mr. Darcy finds hers a face "rendered uncommonly intelligent by the beautiful expression of her dark eyes." Nonetheless, it is this sense of herself as standing apart and watching life which accounts for at least part of Elizabeth's attraction to Mr. Wickham.

Austen has deliberately and obviously made Mr. Wickham a stock character in order to point to Elizabeth's central moral weakness, that she does not take life seriously. Raised by a foolish mother and a cynical father who has abdicated all responsibility, encouraged to distinguish herself from her sisters, Elizabeth sees the world as some sort of entertaining game. She is not silly in the way that Lydia and Kitty are (though she is sometimes surprisingly similar to them), but she cannot imagine that anything could be expected of her. Elizabeth is morally disengaged. What she wants is to understand what she sees and she also hopes that what she sees will be exciting, will be worth understanding. And excitement, of course, is just what she thinks Mr. Wickham offers. His stereotyped charm confers no individual feelings and invokes no personal obligations. His tale is bizarre, out of the ordinary, and shocking, with the initial flattering appeal of being a privileged confidence. It is told to Elizabeth and the reader literally as the recounting of a sentimental story. On Elizabeth's part the hearing is complete with the proper forms of response, with expectations ("what she chiefly wished to hear she could not hope to be told, the history of his acquaintance with Mr. Darcy") and the appropriate stated exclamations (such as "Indeed!", "Good heavens!", "This is quite shocking!", "How strange!", and "How abominable!").

Elizabeth chooses to believe Mr. Wickham's story, and the reason she gives Jane is that "there was truth in his looks." We might accept this as having the familiar meaning that Mr. Wickham has an honest face if it were not that throughout Mr. Wickham's account Austen has Elizabeth think about his good looks. She responds to his declarations of honoring Mr. Darcy's father (declarations made suspect as much by the triteness of their phrasing as by the fact that Mr. Wickham is even now dishonoring the father by exposing Mr. Darcy to Elizabeth) by the remarkable thought that Mr. Wickham was "handsomer than ever as he expressed them." And she silently remarks that Mr. Wickham is a young man "whose very countenance may vouch for [his] being amiable." We cannot simply explain these responses by understanding Elizabeth, as we do Lydia, as a silly and ignorant flirt without any sense. Yet for her the credibility of Mr. Wickham's story is inseparable from his handsome face. Both Mr. Wickham's story and his looks have a glamour which is exceptional and dramatic without being either unpredictable or unique.

Because Austen depicts both Elizabeth's credence and her feelings in the familiar and suspect language of sentimental fiction we must conclude that Elizabeth no more seriously believes Mr. Wickham's tale than she seriously believes she is in love with him. We need only think of how Austen depicts the classic situation of a woman looking forward to seeing a man at a dance. Elizabeth, hoping to see Mr. Wickham at the Netherfield ball, "had dressed with more than usual care, and prepared in the highest spirits for the conquest of all that remained unsubdued of his heart, trusting that it was not more than might be won in the course of the evening." Her own high spirits are the most dominant note here, and when Mr. Wickham does not come, the extent of Elizabeth's real regret may be gauged by Austen's comment that "Elizabeth was not formed for ill-humour; and though every prospect of her own was destroyed for the evening, it could not dwell long on her spirits; and having told all her griefs to Charlotte Lucas, whom she had not seen in a week, she was soon able to make a voluntary transition to the oddities of her cousin." We doubt whether Elizabeth would have found more pleasure in dancing with Mr. Wickham than she does in laughing at Mr. Collins, or whether, indeed, there is finally much difference between the two activities. Both are the expressions of a mind and heart essentially uninvolved. Elizabeth has allowed herself to be taken in by a style which she can later recognize as stale affectation because she views the very artificiality of her connection to Mr. Wickham as an assurance of freedom.

Pride and Prejudice is about a pervasive theme in Austen's work—the charm of what is passing around us, those experiences with other people out of which sound judgment can grow. The particular difficulty preventing proper relationships in *Pride and Prejudice* is the intellectual commitment to a presumed "objectivity," to clarity without involvement. This is the source of Elizabeth's attraction to Mr. Wickham. Her ties to him are as artificial as his character. With Mr. Wickham Elizabeth has played at romance. For Austen the immorality of their relation lies in this fact. Emma must confess to the same empty flirtatiousness, the same vain conduct, in her relations with Frank Churchill. In the terms of *Pride and Prejudice*, there can be nothing between Mr. Wickham and Elizabeth to be grateful for. This is not just a question of distance from emotional involvement. Elizabeth is violating a necessity which is as much a matter of imagination and perception as it is of feelings. Her self-restricting freedom is a refusal to commit her intelligence to growth, to seriousness, to a moral life.

The false choice Elizabeth toys with in her relations to Wickham is taken by and decides the fate of her closest friend, Charlotte Lucas. Descendent of Isabella Thorpe and Lucy Steele and predecessor of Mary Crawford, Charlotte is Austen's first complex portrait of misused sense. Neither Charlotte nor Mary can be dismissed as simply bad. Through Charlotte's wrong way of thinking Austen examines the moral and perceptual consequences of that most alluring of intellectual perspectives to those who think themselves clever: the belief in their own objectivity.

Austen introduces Charlotte as a "sensible, intelligent young woman."

That sense appears in the clear-eyed practicality with which she reflects on her forthcoming marriage: "Mr. Collins to be sure was neither sensible nor agreeable; his society was irksome, and his attachment to her must be imaginary. But still he would be her husband. — Without thinking highly either of men or of matrimony, marriage had always been her object; it was the only honourable provision for well-educated young women of small fortune, and however uncertain of giving happiness, must be their pleasantest preservative from want." As to any question of sensibility, Charlotte quietly tells Elizabeth that "I am not romantic you know. I never was."

These "satisfactory" reflections on having gained her point are untenable. Marriage is not "the only honourable provision" for Charlotte, much as it may be the provision she prefers. We can be sure that honor is not better satisfied by marrying Mr. Collins than by remaining an old maid. Charlotte may, indeed, be right that Mr. Collins offers her the only chance she will have to be married. She is certainly right that it is socially better to be a wife than an unmarried daughter. We need only think of Mr. Woodhouse's gentle gallantry on the precedence of brides. It is socially better — but it is not more honorable. For Charlotte, marriage may be the "pleasantest preservative from want." But living at home at Lucas Lodge she was not, in fact, in want and therefore not at present in need of being preserved from want. Charlotte, of course, was thinking of preserving her future. And when we think of single women who have not done so, we may think of Miss Bates in *Emma*. Her upstairs rooms are small and dreary. But she is neither destitute nor unhappy. Charlotte, choosing "worldly advantage," will get worldly advantage. But she cannot, in defending that choice, justify it by a necessity either economic or social.

Charlotte's decision is immoral. But Austen did not create Charlotte simply to embody her belief that a person should do anything rather than marry without affection. Charlotte's "tolerably composed" reflections about her marriage dramatize a particular attitude of mind. She deceives herself about her motives, and that deception comes from a recognizable intellectual stance which Austen is particularly concerned to expose. Charlotte thinks of herself as a realist, a person who sees life clearly without the distorting haze of feelings and principles. She imagines that she has grown up, that she understands the world, that she has lost her illusions, if she ever had them, and knows what's what. Charlotte's reflections and remarks are characterized by their quietly certain tone and by being generalizations. Charlotte is one of Austen's portraits of sense without sensibility. So too is Lucy Steele. And it should be generally accepted that for Austen there is no sense without sensibility. In a novel about what it means to be intelligent Charlotte is committed to an idea of intelligence which is both insidious and false: she is committed to objectivity without involvement.

Charlotte's defense of her decision to marry Mr. Collins is expressed with the calm certainty of one for whom life holds no surprises and no hope. This certainty is the more remarkable in that it appears in her unstated thoughts. We might expect Charlotte to have a "steady countenance" as she faces the world but, in spite of her discomfort in telling Elizabeth, she knows no doubts in her own mind. Charlotte's certitude places her outside the necessarily continuous activity of human relations. Charlotte is a more mature and more terrifying version of the kind of generalizing fixity of mind Austen has depicted in Marianne Dashwood. Their opinions are opposite. Marianne is all romantic and discomposed. Charlotte is composed and unromantic. But both, having no doubts, have also no possibilities. With that quiet claim of not being romantic Charlotte dismisses not only romance but affection, gratitude, obligation, and the means to human intimacy. Charlotte chooses to marry Mr. Collins because she has no future. To say it another way, Charlotte can imagine a future with Mr. Collins because she cannot imagine a future at all. She can choose "worldly advantage" only because her expectations are so small. "The necessary wisdom for living with Mr. Collins, which Charlotte accepts, is to give up a piece of herself, suppress her shame, lose her ears, see less, diminish her life." Charlotte, the intelligent woman, must relinquish part of her mind.

Elizabeth, talking with Jane of Charlotte's choice of Mr. Collins, says that "the woman who marries him, cannot have a proper way of thinking." And she is precisely right. Charlotte does not have a "proper way of thinking." Truth for Charlotte is not only known but universal. Her impropriety consists in assuming that life holds nothing still to be discovered and in believing that what is known takes the form of abstract generalities. In her satisfactory reflections, Charlotte defends her choice by invoking "the only honourable provision for well-educated young women of small fortune." Charlotte wants to understand the people and events of her life as examples of larger and emptier categories. She wants to understand herself that way as well. We should not overlook the clear echo in Charlotte's invocation of a "single man in possession of a good fortune," the sentence with which Austen opens the book. Charlotte's abstraction, unlike her author's, is without the saving consciousness of irony. For the novel, from that first sentence, is committed to exposing—sometimes comically and sometimes terribly—the emotional sources of such ostensibly general truths. Mary Bennet's aphorisms are a grotesque form of this abstracted point of view.

Charlotte's certainty is really disengaged selfishness and her generalizations are a form of evasiveness which substitutes preconceptions for directly perceiving her life. What Charlotte means by realism, by her calmly practical account of the economics of her decision, is that she did what she had to do. What she means by realism is that she had no choice. Charlotte, invoking the way of the world, diminishes life's possibilities, diminishes herself. Thinking herself free from the blinders of sentiment, she denies her own freedom and responsibility, the power to shape the form of her life. We see the immorality of Charlotte's decision. But because she is not Lucy Steele, because she is intelligent and Elizabeth's friend, what we see most strongly is the waste.

Charlotte's story occurs with Elizabeth's, during the time the novel takes place. Austen offers yet another portrait of a life and mind wasted in Mr. Bennet. While in Charlotte we see how a person makes the self-destructive decision to marry without respect, in Mr. Bennet we see the consequences of such a choice. Mr. Bennet, a man who married a silly woman, is a more developed version of Mr. Palmer in *Sense and Sensibility*, though Mrs. Bennet has not the redeeming kindness of Charlotte Palmer. The weakness of Mr. Bennet, the weakness which must finally make him more culpable than his intolerable wife, is his refusal to be responsible for his life. And we cannot fail to see the connection between Mr. Bennet's kind of intelligence and his culpability. Mr. Bennet, in the novel's famous opening chapter, uses his cleverness to laugh at his wife. We may feel that she deserves it, but we must also recognize that Mr. Bennet's wit is a "breach of conjugal obligation and decorum which, in exposing his wife to the contempt of her own children, [is] so highly reprehensible." Mr. Bennet is a "true philosopher" whose "usual philosophic composure" has much in common with Charlotte Lucas's "tolerable composure." Mr. Bennet also sees himself as a realist, an objective observer of other people's foolishness and self-deceptions. The objectivity of his unbiased cynicism does not except even his own family. Mr. Bennet's steady recognition of Lydia's silliness is unmarred by even a touch of sympathy or of regret that a child of his should have such a nature. He is just as impartial to Jane, and can be amused that she is "crossed in love." Mr. Bennet has failed his family because he has failed his own mind; he has used his intelligence to distance himself from human relations. Retiring to his library, he has retired from his life.

Charlotte Lucas and Mr. Bennet share a life view in which little is expected and disappointment comes as confirmation and relief. Mr. Bennet can be "gratified" to discover that Charlotte is foolish. They take no chances, with their minds or their hearts. Yet these two have been the only intelligent people in Elizabeth's environment and have affected the direction of her mental growth. *Pride and Prejudice* is the story of Elizabeth's movement away from these "sensible" and coldly self-deceptive visions, of releasing her intelligence from defensiveness and negation, and of learning to understand, as Isabel Archer would learn so much more painfully seventy years later, that freedom from significant choices is a prison, that objectivity can be blind, and that to set oneself apart is only to be cut off from the means to truth and to happiness.

Elizabeth, following the disappointments of Mr. Bingley's departure from Netherfield and Charlotte's engagement, responds with a moment of blind cynicism: "There are few people whom I really love, and still fewer of whom I think well. The more I see of the world, the more am I dissatisfied with it; and every day confirms my belief of the inconsistency of all human characters, and of the little dependence that can be placed on the appearance of either merit or sense." Mr. Bennet would approve such remarks. They remind us too of Charlotte's cold and safe conviction that happiness in marriage is "entirely a matter of chance." This closed vision is a violation of Elizabeth's intelligence and an abnegation of her humanity. It is not forced upon her by the vicissitudes of life, being a matter of will rather than circumstance. Her hard opinion of Mr. Bingley's departure makes that clear. That quality in him she had described at Netherfield as the merit "to yield readily—easily—to the *persuasion* of a friend" she now determines to see as "that easiness of temper, that want of proper resolution which now made him the slave of his designing friends." Nor will she mitigate her contempt by recalling Charlotte's warning that Jane's feelings for Bingley were not apparent at all. Elizabeth, seeing herself as the impartial observer, unprejudiced by any feelings toward Bingley, is in fact choosing to place his actions in as bad a light as possible. Such objectivity is nothing less than cynicism. The saving difference between Elizabeth and her father is that her motive is not cool pleasure at the follies of others but a helpless sympathy with her sister's pain.

Perhaps the worst moment of Elizabeth's objectivity is her letter to Mrs. Gardiner telling of Mr. Wickham's defection to Miss King. Her sisters, she says, are more hurt than she for they "are young in the ways of the world, and not yet open to the mortifying conviction that handsome young men must have something to live on, as well as the plain." It is a terrible sentence, terrible in its distance from her feelings, its self-satisfied realism, its "way of the world." And what is most painful is to see Elizabeth choosing to make sense of her experience in such cold and easy terms.

The sense of blasted hopes which passes as a realistic intelligence with Charlotte Lucas and Mr. Bennet is not allowed to influence Elizabeth unchallenged. The cynicism of these two is opposed by a warmer vision, that of Jane Bennet. Elizabeth's "disappointment in Charlotte made her turn with fonder regard to her sister, of whose rectitude and delicacy she was sure her opinion could never be shaken." It is Jane who replies to Elizabeth's despair at human nature and at Charlotte's marriage with the comment, "Do not give way to such feelings as these. They will ruin your happiness." For it is Jane who understands that to view the world coldly is to be neither perceptive nor superior nor safe from wrong. It is to be irresponsible and to abandon the difficulties of trust for the finalities of easy generalization. Jane's prepossession to think well of people does not lead her to be perceptive, and she is obviously wrong about the Bingley sisters. Yet Jane's kind of misunderstanding, unlike the generalizing which presumes certainty, is acceptable to her author in a way that the disposition to think ill of people is not. And her role as the opponent of negativity is central to understanding Elizabeth's mistakes, her choices, and her intellectual growth.

At the beginning of the novel we are assured of Elizabeth's intelligence and Jane's blindness, in part because Elizabeth can see immediately that Bingley's sisters are not well intentioned. And we are quick to think of Jane as sweet but a fool. Although Elizabeth asserts that Jane is so good as to be quite perfect we know she is not. Jane lacks discernment. We are on Elizabeth's side, the side of clarity against softheadedness, as she takes Jane to task with an energy and realism we can only support. We remember the fineness of her reply to Jane's excuses for Charlotte's marriage: "You shall not defend her, though it is Charlotte Lucas. You shall not, for the sake of one individual, change the meaning of principle and integrity, nor endeavour to persuade yourself or me, that selfishness is prudence, and insensibility of danger, security for happiness." And we must be delighted by her answer to Jane's attempt to explain away Mr. Wickham's accusations: "And now, my dear Jane, what have you got to say in behalf of the interested people who have probably been concerned in the business? — Do clear *them* too, or we shall be obliged to think ill of somebody." Against her sister's wit Jane's generous doubts seem foolish indeed. It is in this role of countering Jane's candor that Elizabeth most convinces us of her cleverness and perspicacity.

And yet, in the midst of Elizabeth's lively banter and her quick successes in teasing Jane, there emerges the disturbing fact that her superior wit actually has little to do with truth. Elizabeth may always win the arguments, but she is often wrong. Wickham's story is farfetched, even though Jane cannot sensibly explain why. She is quite right that "one does not know what to think," although the remark does sound limp when followed by Elizabeth's firm "I beg your pardon — one knows exactly what to think." Nor does Jane at all deserve to be accused of subverting principle in explaining Charlotte's marriage, for she attempts to understand Charlotte as much as to excuse her. Elizabeth will not tolerate such an attempt, though a moment before she has found the marriage unaccountable. But it will be Jane who, near the end of the story, pleads with Elizabeth to "do any thing rather than marry without affection." Elizabeth undoubtedly was in the right about the Bingley sisters, but it should be remembered that she had the advantage not only of "more quickness of observation and less pliancy of temper than her sister" but also of a "judgement too unassailed by any attention to herself." Certainly, in the beginning the sisters do treat Jane with more real politeness and kindness than they do Elizabeth. And as Jane herself says, "my confidence was as natural as your suspicion."

Jane's candor, then, is not just the naive blindness Elizabeth would have us believe it to be, any more than Elizabeth's lack of candor is true perception. Indeed, Elizabeth is more than eager to discover and laugh at those faults in others which Jane finds so difficult to see. Moreover, Jane's optimism has to do with her faith that there is much in life that is beyond what she knows and that certainty as to the minds and hearts of others is rare indeed. Elizabeth does not allow for her own ignorance and prefers the certainty of deciding the worst. Her just enjoyment of the follies and nonsense of her companions sometimes goes uncomfortably close to the attitude described by Mr. Darcy as when "the wisest and the best of men, nay, the wisest and best of their actions, may be rendered ridiculous by a person whose first object in life is a joke." For the truth is that both sisters must often judge in ignorance, must imagine, must surmise. But without certain knowledge Elizabeth's lively doubts are no more justified than Jane's candor and gentle trust.

Although the comic side of Jane's goodwill is so delightfully brought out by Elizabeth, its serious value is central to events. On Mr. Wickham's story, "Miss Bennet was the only creature who could suppose there might be any extenuating circumstances in the case, unknown to the society of Hertfordshire; her mild and steady candour always pleaded for allowances, and urged the possiblity of mistakes—but by everybody else Mr. Darcy was condemned as the worst of men." Jane does not see that Mr. Wickham is a liar. But neither does she allow his allegation to subsume her own view of human goodness or her sense of what is probable and likely. In part this is because Jane cannot believe that Mr. Bingley could be so wrong about his friend, Mr. Darcy, and in part because she just cannot conceive of deliberate wrongs. But primarily it is because of Jane's recognition, insisted upon in the face of all Elizabeth's powerful weapons of wit, observation, and laughter, that people and events are more complex and hidden than she can know. Austen has not created Jane as a simple and good-hearted character merely to provide a balance to the complexity and intelligence of her main heroine. When we consider what Jane is doing in the novel and why her author would think her creation neccessary, we must recognize that Jane is by nature neither objective nor perceptive and yet Austen has made her the one character in the novel who is just to Mr. Darcy. By reason of the very qualities which Elizabeth (and the reader) presume to be weaknesses, Jane turns out to be right. Without any "quickness of observation" and with the "wish not to be hasty in censuring anyone," Jane comes closer to truth then her intelligent sister. Certainly, Austen is not instructing us to think pleasant thoughts rather than to apply our powers toward a better understanding of the world. Yet Jane's candor, based on a sense of her own weaknesses, allows a flexibility that Elizabeth lacks.

The willingness to commit oneself to experience, in its unknown dangers as well as its possibilities, comes naturally to Jane, and perhaps that is why she is not the central character of *Pride and Predjudice*. She has never deliberately chosen involvement over clarity. Austen's major interest is always with those whose connections to reality, in terms of knowledge and goodness, are at once more questionable and more difficult. Jane is an innocent. Yet she teaches us that involvement can lead to a kind of perceptiveness inaccessible to those who understand clarity as something gained through avoiding involvement. Elizabeth's freedom, insofar as it leads to judgments she likes to think are untouched by commitment or concern, does not bring understanding. In accounting to Jane for her unfairness to Mr. Darcy, Elizabeth admits that "I meant to be uncommonly clever in taking so decided a dislike to him, without any reason. It is such a spur to one's genius, such an opening for wit to have a dislike of that kind. One may be continually abusive without saying anything just; but one cannot be always laughing at a man without now and then stumbling on something witty." As Catherine Morland had already learned, we are in England, where character is mixed, and that makes it always possible for an observer to find the flaws in others. But to look only for flaws is not objective but selfish and distorting, and cuts oneself off from one's kind. Between candor and cynicism there can be a way of understanding which presupposes neither human evil nor human good, yet allows for both by the very suspension of any fixed view.

During that long walk in the lane at Hunsford Elizabeth offers, for the first time in her story, a picture of her mind at work. The neutral observer, the instant clarity, the conclusive wit, are gone. They must vanish before a dilemma requiring discrimination between versions of a truth she had previously found so clear. Elizabeth moves from feelings "scarcely to be defined" to "feelings yet more acutely painful and more difficult of definition" to a "perturbed state of mind, with thoughts that could rest on nothing" to careful recollections and "pausing on a point a considerable while" to, at last, the realization that "I, who have prided myself on my discernment, . . . have courted prepossession and ignorance, and driven reason away." This scene, comprising a whole chapter, looks forward to Isabel Archer's meditative vigil, the "representation simply of her motionlessly *seeing*," of which James was so proud. In her responses to Darcy's letter Elizabeth does not at all demonstrate that "quickness" her father had praised her for. And that is her victory. Understanding comes slowly, with a depth of feeling Mr. Bennet will never reach in his appreciation of being quick.

One of the most powerful facts in *Pride and Prejudice* is that after Elizabeth's critical moments of shame and revelation at Hunsford so many of her perceptions continue to be quite wrong. She does see through Wickham, but she can learn to detect his artificiality only because she knows the truth. Her judgment not to expose him turns out to be almost disastrous to her own family. And she is still nearly always wrong about Mr. Darcy. She interprets his silence at Lambton on learning of Lydia's elopement with complete assurance: "Her power was sinking; every thing *must* sink under such proof of family weakness, such an assurance of the deepest disgrace. She could neither wonder nor condemn." After Lady Catherine's visit, Elizabeth speculates that if his aunt appeals to Mr. Darcy to give her up, "With his notions of dignity, he would probably feel that the arguments which to Elizabeth had appeared weak and ridiculous, contained much good sense and solid reasoning." Even when all these confusions are resolved by Darcy's second proposal, the two must still spend much of their courtship in the charming yet quite necessary explanations of all those motives and actions so misunderstood. Austen, who did not compose love scenes for their emotional appeal, reminds the reader that in human relations, even of the kind reputed to provide immediate understanding, there is a great deal that intuition and surmise do not reveal.

We must ask what, after all, Elizabeth has learned and what her story is about if after the acknowledgment of prejudice and vanity in the lane at Hunsford her judgment seems hardly more accurate that before. Austen has so arranged the plot that her heroine's moment of revelation and chagrin comes nearly in the middle of the story. After Hunsford there are few scenes of Elizabeth's quickness and wit, and much of the action seems not to depend on her at all. The Gardiners' delayed vacation and wish to visit Pemberley, the combination of Mrs. Forster's invitation, Wickham's mounting debts and Lydia's recklessness which precipitate the elopement, and Mr. Darcy's arrival at the Lambton inn at the moment of Elizabeth's receiving the news, all remind us that Elizabeth can have little control over people or events, while both may be crucial to her. The second half of *Pride and Prejudice* may be less sparkling than the first, but the quieter pleasure it offers is an extended view of Elizabeth's fate entwined with the lives of those around her.

What Elizabeth is doing in these later scenes, with a directness and care which were absent from her earlier casual wit, is seriously trying to understand the particular situations she finds herself in and the people she cares about. This effort is given more space in *Pride and Prejudice* than it was in *Northanger Abbey* or will be in *Emma*. By placing Elizabeth's moment of crisis in the middle of the novel rather than at the end, Austen can present Elizabeth as a heroine who needs to be educated and also as a heroine who is properly involved in her world. Whether she is trying to compose her feelings enough at the Lambton inn to receive Georgiana Darcy and her brother, or paying a morning visit to the ladies at Pemberley, or accepting what she believes to be Darcy's giving her up after the elopement, or speculating (with the Gardiners and Jane) on Mr. Wickham's intentions, or surmising Mr. Darcy's reaction to his aunt's interference, Elizabeth is constantly engaged in trying to see and respond to other points of view. She is often wrong—and for quite the same reasons that she was wrong in the beginning, that her partialities and ignorance must limit her. The difference is that Elizabeth no longer sees her world as a place of easily discovered folly from which, in self-defence as much as in amusement, she must stand apart if she is to see the truth. She has come to value the connections and partialities which inform truth and to understand the lesson of Hunsford, that a lively intelligence is personal and engaged. She can now use that quick mind to reach for hopes and suggestive meanings rather than killing finalities. The former view had placed Elizabeth, along with her father, among those who understand human nature in crude categories of behavior and motivation. Against this reductive view Austen places a vision of people as palpable yet flexible and elusive beyond our predictions for them. And even Jane's candor is not so conclusively defined as to be unchanged by Miss Bingley's unkindness.

Like Emma, as Elizabeth learns to suspend judgment and examine her experience, she also becomes aware of her own affections. She knew from the time of the Hunsford visit that her opinion of Mr. Darcy had been wrong. Yet her most important lesson concerning him is not that he is good but that he loves her in ways that can overcome the failings in his character. Lydia Bennet's elopement with Mr. Wickham is a curiously obtrusive event in an Austen novel. Yet it is through this terrible act that Elizabeth realizes her obligation to Mr. Darcy, an obligation which, as he makes clear, could only have come about because he loves her. All was done for Elizabeth's sake. And it is a romantic moment for these most unromantic lovers when Elizabeth finally expresses her obligation and finds herself being proposed to. Elizabeth's gratitude—gratitude in the sense in which Austen means it—is not for a favor done, not for an act of socially right behavior. It is a gratitude that, despite all the obstacles which reality can provide, despite time, conventions, and misunderstandings, despite her wrongs and his limitations, Mr. Darcy can see her honestly and love her as well.

Between these lovers there are no longer any of the conventional dangers of social slips or sudden reversals of opinion, as there always were in Elizabeth's relations with Wickham. That is why Mr. Darcy's proposal would have come without Elizabeth's offered thanks or without Lady Catherine's interference. Their feelings are past being subject to the accidents of circumstance. Fate is an empty convention of romance. Instead, Mr. Darcy offers Elizabeth an understanding of herself, one that is moral and affectionate and sound. It is a vision of clarity because of his involvement, a vision from a generous heart. To recognize that and to appreciate it is a reciprocal feeling which will unite Elizabeth with Mr. Darcy. For gratitude is an act of self-love which carries with it an act of love.

Near the end of the novel Mr. Bingley returns to Hertfordshire and rides into the paddock at Longbourn. Mrs. Bennet, seeing him from her window, calls to her daughters to come as well. "Jane resolutely kept her place at the table; but Elizabeth, to satisfy her mother, went to the window — she looked, — she saw Mr. Darcy with him, and sat down again by her sister." With this image of the two sisters, and Elizabeth's gesture of looking changed to shared embarrassment and retreat, Austen captures her heroine's transformation from a detached to an engaged vision. Elizabeth discovers that clarity is not immediate, that even revelations are a matter of changing feelings and a matter of time.

The Comedy of Manners

Jan Fergus

The usual definition of the comedy of manners derives from Restoration comedy: "this form deals with the relations and intrigues of gentlemen and ladies living in a polished and sophisticated society, evokes laughter mainly at the violations of social conventions and decorum, and relies for its effect in great part on the wit and sparkle of the dialogue." This general definition ignores, as it must, the achievement of the best works in the genre (such as *The Way of the World*) in which true wit and good manners serve to define the characters' worth in the world they inhabit. An analogous use of manners to indicate morals, especially in such actions as Mr. Knightley's asking Harriet Smith to dance in *Emma* or, conversely, Emma's rudeness to Miss Bates, is frequently noticed and much admired in Austen's novels, though sometimes with an implication that the device is common or conventional, however extraordinary the handling. But models for these incidents are not to be found in the social comedy of novelists who precede Austen. Even Burney and Richardson treat social comedy or the comedy of manners in a way that illuminates Austen's achievement and her mastery, instead of anticipating it, despite a few exceptions in *Sir Charles Grandison*.

The comedy of manners is a literary convention which depends very much on highly-developed and codified social convention, not simply for its material (the "manners" of a period), but for its significance: its ability to embody in comic confrontations important differences between characters and distinct evaluations of them ("morals"). The social conventions supporting the literary convention must ideally be serious as well as elaborate. The behaviour dictated by social conventions must invite scrutiny and must reward it, so that description of social

From *Jane Austen and the Didactic Novel*: Northanger Abbey, Sense and Sensibility, *and* Pride and Prejudice. ©1983 by Jan Fergus. Barnes & Noble, Totowa, New Jersey, 1983.

conduct can be a reliable index to character. Such description has at the same time another function, and one more usually associated with the comedy of manners; the recording of a particular social milieu. This wider and essentially simpler use of the convention, while important, does not serve to define Austen's differences from her predecessors as clearly as does the other use which the convention permits: the possibility of indicating the grossest and most minute discriminations among characters. For in Austen's novels, as [Jane] Nardin claims, "All deviations from [the code of propriety] have a meaning; all reveal something about character"; and her study carefully documents the complex ways that Austen uses "social behavior" as the "external manifestation" of a character's "internal moral and psychological condition."

Before Austen, the comedy of manners when adapted to the novel form tends to make only rather gross discriminations among manners and characters. Burney, for example, describes extremes of vulgarity, affectation, and naiveté, and she exhibits these extremes in comic confrontations with each other and with polite behaviour. As a result, although she may distinguish between various forms of affectation (in *Cecilia*, among the sects of the "supercilious," "voluble," "jargonists," and "insensiblists," so classified by Mr. Gosport at the Pantheon assembly), she does not similarly distinguish differences in polite behaviour. Instead, she takes polite behaviour for granted, or at least is not interested in particularizing it. In Burney's novels, good breeding is portrayed in chiaroscuro: it can shine by contrast only, and one result of this technique is that Burney's ballrooms and drawing-rooms are overstocked with vulgarians. Samuel Johnson highly approved this technique. The vulgarians who delighted him so much in *Evelina* are, in his view, successful only because they shine by contrast. Burney has recorded his pronouncement that the "comic humour of character . . . owes its effect to contrast; for without Lord Orville, and Mr. Villars, and that melancholy and gentleman-like half-starved Scotchman, poor Macartney, the Brangtons, and the Duvals, would be less than nothing; for vulgarity, in its own unshadowed glare, is only disgusting." Johnson evidently does not regret that the comedy of manners in Burney's novels is always raucous, and never aims at or allows those fine discriminations between well-bred men and women that Richardson and Austen deal with.

Richardson's interest in drawing fine distinctions among characters is obsessive, but even in *Sir Charles Grandison* he does not rely on conventionally good manners to indicate moral stature. He is eager, first, to portray the manners of "high life" accurately, in order to offer through his exemplary characters some prescriptions of his own for truly polite behaviour. He must therefore show himself and his characters to be familiar with the conventional code of manners, not violating it. But since he was not familiar with the more minute or stylized conventions of good society, he relied on his "polite" correspondents to correct details of social usage in his novels. A prescriptive attitude toward conduct or manners is characteristic of Richardson and his audience, and is thus very prominent in his novels. This prescriptiveness distinguishes Richardson's concern with accuracy in presenting the minutiae of manners from Austen's. She is concerned that every detail she includes be correct. She revised inexact detail of this sort (for example, introducing a country surgeon to a lord) in her niece Anna's manuscript novel. But she does not share Richardson's didacticism about manners: whatever didactic intentions she has, Austen makes no effort to prescribe the manners or conduct appropriate to every occasion of domestic life. When Richardson writes to a correspondent (who is actually urging him to extend *Grandison* beyond its seven volumes) that, "By what we have seen of *both* [Sir Charles and Harriet], we know how they will behave on every future call or occasion," it is only too true.

Richardson does explore at least one serious and elaborate social form for his social comedy, the compliment, a form Austen's novels also exploit from time to time. Mr. Collins's "little elegant compliments as may be adapted to ordinary occasions" typify her broadly comic attitude in the early novels, while the treatment of compliments in *Emma* is incalculably more complex. Differences in manners, and more, are registered, and assist in defining the characters who are exposed to them as well as those responsible for them. Furthermore, all the concern with flattery and compliments culminates, like so much in the novel, in Mr. Knightley's proposal: "I cannot make speeches, Emma." The powerful emotional and thematic significance Austen can extract from so (apparently) insignificant a social form, while preserving a comic tone throughout, becomes even more astonishing when compared to Richardson's similar attempt in *Grandison*. His (and his characters') scrutiny of compliments and the motives behind them becomes so serious, so anxious, so full of meaning, so obsessive finally, that comedy is undermined. The obsessiveness insists only too much on the connection between manners and morals, so that comic confrontations and comic release are nearly impossible.

This obsession with compliments might be expected from an author who was notoriously greedy for praise and who died, according to Samuel Johnson, "merely for want of change among his flatterers." In justice to Richardson's intense concern with ulterior motives for compliments, his early exposure to the disingenuousness which can underlie conventional formulae should be remembered. In his biographical letter to Johannes Stinstra he reveals that at thirteen he was party to ladies' "Love Secrets" and was writing letters for them: "I have been directed to chide, & even repulse, when an Offence was either taken or given, at the very time that the Heart of the Chider or Repulser was open before me, overflowing with Esteem & Affection; & the fair Repulser dreading to be taken at her Word." Richardson's tone is light, but still registers the same consciousness of deception and awareness of the need for self-protection which accompany analyses of compliments in *Grandison*, qualifying the comic incongruities revealed. Thus Harriet, having arrived in London, recalls her friends' wishes that she will acquaint them with all the admiration she receives, and her uncle's comment that "The vanity of the Sex . . . will not suffer any thing of this sort to escape our Harriet." She is led from this lightness immediately to a serious reflection, the first of several on the subject:

> It is true, my Lucy, that we young women are too apt to be pleased with the admiration *pretended* for us by the other Sex. But I have always endeavour'd to keep down any foolish pride of this sort, by such considerations as these: That flattery is the vice of men: That they seek to raise us in order to lower us, and in the end to exalt themselves on the ruins of the pride they either hope to find, or inspire: That humility, as it shines brightest in an high condition, best becomes a flatter'd woman of all women: That she who is puffed up by the praises of men, on the supposed advantages of person, answers *their end* upon her; and seems to own, that she thinks it a principal part of *hers*, to be admired by them: And what can give more importance to them, and less to herself, than this?

This analysis of men's motives in paying compliments, and the dangers women run in accepting them, is only preliminary. The form of a compliment, the manner of its delivery, and above all the manner of its reception, are felt to supply significant information about the characters responsible for them: about their manners, their perception, even at times their moral worth. This social form *can* serve, then, as a reliable index to character in Richardson's novels, and the main characters, who so often hear their own praises, are very much aware that this is so. They therefore feel a need for careful calculation and scrutiny of their responses to compliments. When Lady Betty, a new acquaintance in London, claims that she expects to be "equally delighted and improved" by Harriet's company, Harriet is wary:

> I bowed in silence. I love not to make disqualifying speeches; by such we seem to intimate that we believe the complimenter to be in earnest, or perhaps that we think the compliment our due, and want to hear it either repeated or confirmed; and yet, possibly, we have not that pretty confusion, and those transient blushes, ready, which Mr. Greville archly says are always to be at hand when we affect to disclaim the

attributes given us.

Lady Betty was so good as to stop there; tho' the muscles of her agreeable face shewed a polite promptitude, had I, by disclaiming her compliments, provok'd them to perform their office.

This interaction is complex. Even between women, the giving and receiving of compliments may be a snare for vanity and manipulation. When compliments occur between men and women, however, the stakes are higher, for compliments are prescribed in two antithetical social contexts: they belong to formal courtship ("paying addresses"), and they belong to gallantry and coquetry, what Richardson calls "polite raillery," and what "no English word but flirtation could very well describe," as Austen puts it in *Emma*. Serious "intentions" or mere mockery may lie behind a compliment, but in either case, the conventional stance of the person who receives it is disbelief, a stance which may compromise one's sincerity and in any case asks for a repetition of the offence. Harriet's response when Sir Hargrave proposes to her sheds some interesting light on the resulting intricacy of these forms:

> I would have played a little female trifling upon him, and affected to take his professions only for polite raillery, which men call *making love* to young women, who perhaps are frequently but too willing to take in earnest what the wretches mean but in jest; but the fervour with which he *renewed* (as he called it) his declaration, admitted not of fooling; and yet his *volubility* might have made questionable the sincerity of his declarations. As therefore I could not think of encouraging his addresses, I thought it best to answer him with openness and unreserve.

Pretended disbelief, or "trifling," would be in order only if Harriet were planning to encourage Sir Hargrave. The exchanges of compliments that form the surface of polite conversation in Richardson's novels and which are, above all, required in the encounters of men and women, are an extremely complex social form, whose complexity derives from the conflicting motives it can accommodate. Sincerity, insincerity, perception, consideration, deviousness, vanity, hypocrisy, vulgarity, delicacy, manipulation—all these may be contained within and revealed below the smooth surface of the forms of polite admiration. Thus these forms seem to be ideal for "serious" comedy, the comedy of manners which reveals character.

Richardson does extract from the forms some comedy of this sort, as when Sir Hargrave is introduced:

> for he forgets not to pay his respects to himself at every glass; yet does it with a seeming consciousness, as if he would hide a vanity too apparent

to be concealed; breaking from it, if he finds himself observed, with an half-careless, yet seemingly dissatisfied air, pretending to have discover'd something amiss in himself. This seldom fails to bring him a compliment: Of which he shews himself very sensible, by affectedly disclaiming the merit of it; perhaps with this speech, bowing, with his spread hand on his breast, waving his head to and fro—By my soul, Madam (or Sir) you do me too much honour.

Such a man is Sir Hargrave Pollexfen. . . . He would have it that I was a perfect beauty, and he supposed me very young—Very silly of course: And gave himself such airs, as if he were sure of my admiration.

I viewed him steadily several times; and my eye once falling under his, as I was looking at him, I dare say, he at that moment pity'd the poor fond heart, which he supposed was in tumults about him; when, at the very time I was considering, whether, if I were obliged to have the one or the other, as a punishment for some great fault I had committed, my choice would fall on Mr. Singleton, or on him.

Harriet's observations and attitudes must have delighted Austen. In *Emma*, the heroine's attitude toward Mr. Elton similarly combines close observation with ironic reflection. When Mr. Elton praises Emma's drawing, her "inimitable figure-pieces," Emma's thoughts indicate her own amused detachment but her response feeds his vanity, as Harriet Byron's does Sir Hargrave's: "Yes, good man! —thought Emma—but what has all that to do with taking likenesses? You know nothing of drawing. Don't pretend to be in raptures about mine. Keep your raptures for Harriet's face. 'Well, if you give me such kind encouragement, Mr. Elton, I believe I shall try what I can do.'" Such examples show Austen's comedy to be more powerful than Richardson's even at his best, not simply because she dramatizes it more, the usual explanation. She learns in *Mansfield Park* and *Emma* to make each incident express more and more comic or emotional incongruity. Emma's delusions about Mr. Elton's love for Harriet Smith, which spring from her own vanity, complicate this incident and create in the reader a combination of distance with engagement that Richardson's account of Harriet and Sir Hargrave does not demand.

The major difference between Richardson's and Austen's treatment of social forms, and particularly of "polite raillery," is that, in this context at least, Richardson lacks a sense of play. He can allow Harriet's relations with Sir Hargrave to be amusing at first because Sir Hargrave is a fool, and Harriet is in no danger of being attracted to him. When he becomes the villain who has abducted Harriet, he can no longer be treated comically, and should not be; but Richardson's impulse to turn folly into villainy is characteristic. Sir Hargrave's future role in the action is predictable to anyone familiar with Richardson's work: having become the stock libertine, he pursues his unregenerate courses until he reaches a penitent death-bed. Richardson usually finds the relations between men and women either too threatening or else too easily assimilated to the conventions of melodrama for him to sustain a comic or playful tone. He is serious when he allows Sir Charles to say, "Men and women are Devils to one another. They need no other tempter." *Grandison* begins as if Richardson can treat relations between the sexes comically, but Harriet's suitors soon become pathetic rather than comic, and her vanity, wit, and social life decline as she falls in love, so that only characters who are almost uniformly good remain, and Richardson could not allow them to be coquettes. Austen is perfectly capable of exploring and rendering all the wilfulness or ugliness that can lie behind flirtation, as is evident in her treatment of the relations between Julia and Maria Bertram and Henry Crawford in *Mansfield Park*, or in her treatment of Frank Churchill and Emma at Box Hill. She is, however, equally capable of a number of other attitudes toward flirtation, ranging from her detached ridicule of its mindless vanity in Kitty and Lydia Bennet to her playful delight in Elizabeth's having "dressed with more than usual care" for the ball at Netherfield and having "prepared in the highest spirits for the conquest of all that remained unsubdued of [Wickham's] heart, trusting that it was not more than might be won in the course of the evening."

Just as Richardson's attitude toward manners in his comedy generally lacks Austen's sense of play, his inclusion of revealing gestures in manner lacks her sense of structure. Although in *Grandison* he declares that in "small instances . . . are the characters of the heart displayed, far more than in greater" and in his letters that "in the minutiae lie often the unfoldings of the Story, as well as of the heart," his minutiae are essentially decorative, not structural: they create no real consequences for the plot. The "small instance" he refers to is typical. Sir Charles, having rather abruptly left his circle in the drawing-room, takes the first opportunity to return, in order to explain that he is not really angry with anyone. The incident is edifying, not moving, and not important to the plot. It simply shows Sir Charles's moral virtue in yet another context. Austen, however, actually invents the "illustrative" or characteristic gesture in manner which is also emotionally resonant or structural or both. Mr. Knightley's asking Harriet to dance, to take the most famous example, is all three. It illustrates his character, including his complete superiority to Mr. Elton. It relieves a painfully embarrassing situation, for Harriet, Mrs. Weston, Emma, and the reader; it also permits Emma to ask Mr. Knightley to dance with her later, an incident highly charged with emotion because of Emma's unconscious love for him and his conscious love for her, which he thinks unrequited. Finally, the incident has important consequences for the plot by allowing

Harriet to think herself in love with Mr. Knightley, a development vital to the climax: Emma's discovery of her love for Mr. Knightley and their subsequent engagement. Few gestures even in Austen's novels are so significant, but those less embedded in plot can also have great power, as when in *Mansfield Park* Edmund Bertram gives Fanny Price a gold chain, or Sir Thomas orders her a fire although angry with her.

The sense of play and sense of structure which Austen brings to her treatment of manners invests them with comic, emotional, moral and thematic content that her predecessors cannot attain. Her finest achievements in this mode occur in the later novels, although *Pride and Prejudice* foreshadows some of the later mastery of small, significant incident when Elizabeth unconventionally walks cross-country to visit Jane, when Lady Catherine keeps Charlotte Collins outside by her carriage, or when Darcy is silent and thoughtful at Longbourn near the end. These incidents, although they point to Austen's later development, do not fully anticipate it.

The best effects in *Pride and Prejudice* are achieved because Austen experiments with and masters other elements in the comedy of manners: wit and dialogue. The two are distinct, though sometimes confused. Dialogue may or may not be witty, while wit need not form part of anything deserving the name of dialogue, which implies reciprocity: at least in some sense, ideas and opinions are being exchanged among reasonably attentive speakers, not merely displayed by them.

Whether wit appears in dialogue, so understood, or not, an author can count on favourable responses to it and to characters responsible for it, since pleasure in well-phrased judgments or criticisms, and in perceptions or exposures of incongruity, is essentially an intellectual rather than a moral response. If wit is to be registered as anything but delightful, extremely skilful treatment is needed, like that in *Mansfield Park* and *Emma*. Once Mr. Knightley has rebuked Emma for the witty remark to Miss Bates she "could not resist" making, an engaged reader must feel shock, embarrassment, and even horror at Emma's wit. Austen's treatment makes her remark then seem anything but witty. In *Pride and Prejudice*, her demands on the reader's emotions in response to wit are less complex and less strenuous, for her interest lies primarily in a more easily-handled theme. She exposes the imperception rather than the ugliness which pleasure in wit can produce. Nevertheless, she does demand that the reader register the inaccuracies of judgment encouraged by Elizabeth's wit. In her treatment of Mr. Bennet, she requires a yet more complex response.

In chapter 2, Mr. Bennet's wit displays this contempt for his wife and provokes her to expose herself before their children. Austen inserts this scene as a possible check to the reader's simple delight in Elizabeth's wit even before that delight can occur, for Elizabeth says nothing remarkable until chapter 4. Although chapter 2 is composed almost entirely of speeches, they do not constitute real dialogue. Mr. and Mrs. Bennet talk at cross-purposes. Mrs. Bennet is wholly oblivious to her husband's mockery, but neither her idiocy nor her blindness can excuse him. Mr. Bennet's wit seldom appears in dialogue whatever his company, for his ironic detachment usually precludes it. At the Netherfield ball, for example, he puts a stop to Mary's indifferent singing with an isolated remark, "That will do extremely well, child. You have delighted us long enough. Let the other young ladies have time to exhibit." When Elizabeth tries to persuade him to prevent Lydia's going to Brighton, he replies, "Lydia will never be easy till she has exposed herself in some public place or other, and we can never expect her to do it with so little expense or inconvenience to her family as under the present circumstances." This remark is as irresponsible as it is amusing. It is also firmly attached to the plot, for in Brighton Lydia does expose herself: she elopes with Wickham, an action that brings about the denouement. The rest of the scene between Elizabeth and her father counterpoints her earnestness with his irresponsibility. Although in speaking to Elizabeth Mr. Bennet can be serious, even affectionate, his detachment and withdrawal usually operate even then. His only "dialogue" occurs at the end, when he appeals to Elizabeth to reconsider her engagement. Moved as he is in the scene, he quickly resumes his ironic stance once assured that Elizabeth loves Darcy.

Wit is, fortunately, more a part of dialogue in *Pride and Prejudice* than separable from it. Nothing could be more tedious, however, than dialogue (or narrative for that matter) composed entirely of epigrams, as some of George Meredith's novels too frequently testify. Although Austen herself refers to the "epigrammatism of the general style," she has taken care that most of the wit be thematically significant and resonant beyond whatever immediate effect it creates. And the wit which she embeds in dialogue is at least as immediately delightful as Mr. Bennet's and has far more complex uses in controlling the reader's response to the characters. The popular judgment that dialogue is the great achievement of *Pride and Prejudice* is certainly correct, although admiration is usually confined to its wit and its success in revealing character. Besides its entertaining and dramatic qualities, however, the witty dialogue among groups of characters in *Pride and Prejudice* gives fuller expression to feeling, perception, and judgment, and consequently to the themes, than the dialogue of *Sense and Sensibility* and *Northanger Abbey* permits or intends. Without relinquishing earlier techniques of dialogue, Austen experiments with a number of new ones which allow increased expressiveness and which demand increasingly complex responses from readers. In *Mansfield Park, Emma,* and *Persuasion*, the characters' talk is so much more carefully orchestrated and highly organized than in *Pride and*

Prejudice that it should be distinguished by a more suggestive and wider term than dialogue: conversation. The conversations in the later novels are created by techniques fully evident in the dialogues of *Pride and Prejudice* but used with greater selectivity, density, and economy, and thus with greater power.

One form of dialogue visible in *Pride and Prejudice* and *Sense and Sensibility* but eliminated later is a legacy from the eighteenth-century novel and supplies social comedy narrowly defined. A number of speakers expose their characteristic faults or foibles by their various responses to a particular event or topic. This form is very common in *Pride and Prejudice*. Chapter 5, containing the five-way debate on pride, is a typical example. Some critics cite scenes like this one as evidence that Austen adopts a kind of relativism, but "relativistic impressionism" is hardly her aim. For her, and for the eighteenth century in general, human motives are fathomable, however, complex; human judgments are corrigible, however prone to error; and human misconduct can be understood as folly and vice, not as their modern counterparts, neurosis and a secularized notion of original sin. Austen inherits a comic tradition which assumes that a complete, instructive, and morally useful picture of society can be obtained by bringing together characters who exhibit manners, follies, and affectations carefully chosen to contrast with each other as much as possible. The plays of Congreve and the novels of Fielding and Burney supply social comedy or the comedy of manners in this narrow sense. The form has undeniable virtues. It allows fools like Mrs. Bennet to expose their folly with wonderful economy, while wits like Elizabeth shine by comparison. It can even be used if the follies of rational characters are to be displayed, as in *Sense and Sensibility* when Marianne's amusing notion that Colonel Brandon at thirty-five is too old and infirm to love is contrasted with the more accurate views of Mrs. Dashwood and Elinor. But the broad, glaring contrasts essential to this form of dialogue disqualify it for the finer discriminations among feelings, perceptions, and judgments which are Austen's major interest and which the new techniques of *Pride and Prejudice* accommodate.

These new techniques may be divided into two classes according to the effects they produce on the reader. First, effects may be immediate, and will depend on what the reader knows that the characters do not. Or effects may be delayed, and will depend on what the reader either can know but for various reasons does not realize (e.g., that Wickham's account of Darcy is fake), or what he simply cannot know until a later point in the novel or until a second reading. A good example of this last class is linear irony which does not stem directly from Elizabeth's misunderstanding of Darcy and Wickham: Elizabeth's shock at Charlotte's engagement set against Jane's later shock at Elizabeth's. The difference between this sort of linear irony and earlier structural ironies in Austen's work is interesting. The discussion of Colonel Brandon's "infirmity" in *Sense and Sensibility* does create structural irony, for Marianne, having thought that Colonel Brandon, "if he were ever animated enough to be in love, must have long outlived every sensation of the kind," marries him at last, although he is a man "whom, two years before, she had considered too old to be married — and who still sought the constitutional safeguard of a flannel waistcoat." In this instance, irony produces a comic effect independent of the novel's thematic concern with distinguishing sensitive, considerate behaviour from insensitivity and self-indulgence. In *Pride and Prejudice*, however, ironies of structure recur and are intimately connected with the theme, humbling pride of judgment.

Austen's ability to make dialogue serve her themes is not confined to the delayed effects supplied by linear irony or by such *tours de force* as Wickham's first conversations with Elizabeth. Most of the dialogue in *Pride and Prejudice* creates immediate effects, either those comic effects typical of eighteenth-century social comedy, or more complex ones which depend on what the reader knows that the characters do not. These complex effects are both emotional and comic. They increase in power the more the reader "knows" — the more attention he pays — and are Austen's signature and her triumph. The reader has every incentive to read closely, for the more he is aware of the characters' motives, reactions, and misconceptions, the funnier the comedy. And the perfect lucidity with which unstated emotions and judgments display themselves to an attentive reader gives him that illusion of engagement with life which great art always produces by being clear, highly organized, and complex where life is opaque and incoherent. *Pride and Prejudice* is a great work insofar as its brilliant lucidity transcends the complexity of life. But it is a puzzling and even flawed work if compared to Austen's later novels, insofar as its lucidity can also be excessive and glaring, violating life. When Austen writes mere social comedy, like that of chapter 5, character is necessarily simplified, for the effect depends on broad contrasts; characters merely personify different manners and attitudes. Such comedy is too lucid. When Austen writes her own higher comedy in *Pride and Prejudice*, she succeeds in permitting characters to expose, beneath the surface restraints of polite, clever talk, their unstated and incongruous (or clashing) motives, judgments, and feelings. The range of comic and emotional incongruity which Austen learns to make her dialogue convey and her readers perceive in *Pride and Prejudice* is nicely illustrated, on the one hand, by the early scenes at Netherfield and, on the other, by Darcy's first proposal to Elizabeth.

The dialogues at Netherfield reveal incongruities in manners, motives, and judgments which the reader registers as largely comic, although discrepancies and incongruities in feeling inevitably accompany them. This form of dialogue never permits merely comic incongruity; emotional incongruity always complicates the comedy. Sometimes, indeed, emotional incongruity is the source of comedy: the discrepancy between Miss Bingley's interest in Darcy and his perfect indifference to her is wholly comic, as is Miss Bingley's jealousy of Elizabeth. The discrepancy between Darcy's interest in Elizabeth and her dislike is, however, more complex in its effects. When Darcy and Elizabeth identify each other's faults of character, the scene is principally comic, for each complacently misunderstands the other's meaning and motives, and the reader knows more than either can. Such comedy is central to the themes and plot of the novel, for Darcy's fault is "a propensity to hate every body" and Elizabeth's "wilfully to misunderstand them." Yet the scene has undercurrents of sexual antagonism and attraction not entirely contained by the comedy of misjudgment enacted on the surface or by the linear irony which allows Elizabeth's and Darcy's judgments of each other to be felt again and again throughout the novel.

This form of dialogue, the source of what may be called Austen's high comedy, is perfectly illustrated by the scene which takes up the first half of chapter 10. The dialogue opens comically, develops emotional undertones and thematic implications through a variety of new techniques, and ends with a higher, more complex comedy than anything promised by its beginning. Austen prefaces this scene by noting that Darcy is writing to his sister, Miss Bingley is praising his efforts, and Elizabeth is "sufficiently amused" by their "curious dialogue, . . . exactly in unison with her opinion of each." The reader should allow this observation to guide his understanding of the entire scene. He should notice that nothing Darcy says shakes Elizabeth's opinion of his pride, conceit, and ill temper. The dialogue is so skilfully contrived, however, that while a prejudiced mind, like Elizabeth's, can see these qualities in Darcy's remarks, an open mind will not. When Darcy replies to Miss Bingley's inane question, "do you always write such charming long letters," with "They are generally long; but whether always charming, it is not for me to determine," a reader can take its politely repelling irony as evidence that Darcy, neither seeking nor liking Miss Bingley's flattery, puts up with it and her remarkably well. The reader, of course, is better able than Elizabeth to interpret Darcy's behaviour correctly, having information she has not: that Darcy is attracted to Elizabeth and is as well-acquainted with Miss Bingley's jealousy as with her designs on him. These emotions have been amply demonstrated by Darcy's earlier pointed (but still polite) rebuke to Miss Bingley's catty remarks about Elizabeth: "there is meanness in *all* the arts which ladies sometimes condescend to employ for captivation. Whatever bears affinity to cunning is despicable." Yet ambiguity is not entirely dispelled by such speeches. A reader can take Darcy's remarks here and in chapter 10 as Elizabeth would: evidence of ill-mannered conceit. His appreciation of the finer comedy in these scenes is simply delayed, and the immediate effect for him is purely comic. But it ought to be more complex. The reader should be able to see Darcy as politely, forbearingly ironic in his reception of Miss Bingley's officious compliments and should be aware that Elizabeth is viewing the same behaviour as evidence of his rudeness and his pride. Thus, the reader is asked to respond at several levels.

If the reader fails to be conscious of these incongruities, they are felt at last as linear ironies in the novel's comic attack on pride of judgment. The unconscious reader is but the more closely implicated. At the close of *Pride and Prejudice*, Elizabeth is able to reinterpret Darcy's behaviour, explicitly recognizing what she would not see earlier, although she could have seen it, as should the reader. She tells Darcy, "You were disgusted with the women who were always speaking and looking, and thinking for *your* approbation alone." Linear irony allows Austen to create comedy in which nothing is lost.

As the scene in chapter 10 progresses, its demands on the reader increase. Miss Bingley's flattery peaks: "a person who can write a long letter, with ease, cannot write ill." Bingley is moved to interrupt with the first of several jokes he makes in this scene at Darcy's expense: "That will not do for a compliment to Darcy . . . because he does *not* write with ease. He studies too much for words of four syllables. — Do not you, Darcy?" A dramatization of Bingley's and Darcy's friendship follows. Their affectionate exchange could modify Elizabeth's earlier judgment that Darcy "was only the man who made himself agreeable no where," but does not. The reader must register her obliviousness while he takes in the two men's friendly, bantering discussion of Bingley's character, to which Elizabeth contributes twice. This discussion begins with a casual reference to essential differences between Bingley and Darcy. Darcy remarks that his style of writing is "very different" from Bingley's. Miss Bingley cites her brother's careless and blotted letters, and he declares, "My ideas flow so rapidly that I have not time to express them—by which means my letters sometimes convey no ideas at all to my correspondents." Elizabeth takes the opportunity to praise Bingley for his humility, a quality she believes that Darcy conspicuously lacks. The reader should observe that all Elizabeth's speeches in this scene show her to be preoccupied with Darcy's character and with a desire to goad him. Darcy will not let her comment pass, observing that the "appearance of humility . . . is often only carelessness of opinion, and sometimes an indirect boast." This Johnsonian distinction amuses Bingley: "And which of the two do you call *my* little recent piece of modesty?" Darcy's reply analyzes Bingley's character in a friendly, intimate, but also formal style: "you are really proud of your defects in writing. . . . When you told Mrs. Bennet this morning that if you ever resolved on quitting Netherfield you should be gone in five minutes, you meant it to be a sort of panegyric, of compliment to yourself—and yet what is there so very laudable in a precipitance which must leave very necessary business undone, and can be of no real advantage to yourself or any one else?" Two new techniques of dialogue become apparent here. Austen allows her characters to refer to earlier conversations. And she allows the characters to debate as well as dramatize the central issue: judgment of character, in this case, Bingley's. The effects of these techniques are best understood, however, in relation to the entire scene, whose tensions increase enormously from this point.

Bingley's reply to Darcy's analysis is amused and friendly in tone, but after an initial laugh over remembering "at night all the foolish things that were said in the morning," becomes rather self-justifying. He would, he says, leave Netherfield as quickly as he had claimed, and so "did not assume the character of needless precipitance merely to shew off before the ladies." Darcy, as a friend will, pursues his advantage. He is "by no means convinced" that Bingley would leave so readily: "if, as you were mounting your horse, a friend were to say, 'Bingley, you had better stay till next week,' you would probably do it, you would probably not go—and, at another word, might stay a month." At this point, the witty exchange between Darcy and Bingley has acquired a slight edge audible to an attentive reader, but the tone remains good-humoured. Although Darcy claims to know Bingley better than he does himself, in another sense both men understand each other perfectly. The comedy of this section arises from the discrepancy between their intimacy and Elizabeth's obliviousness to it. She sees Bingley's sweetness without his amusement at Darcy, and Darcy's arrogance without his affection for Bingley. She believes herself to see more than either, as her next remark shows. She tells Darcy, "You have only proved by this . . . that Mr. Bingley did not do justice to his own disposition. You have shewn him off now much more than he did himself." Once again, she is eager to praise Bingley for a quality she thinks lacking in Darcy, but more important, she gives a new and complex turn to the dialogue by addressing Darcy directly and rather accusingly. From this point, Darcy's character is openly discussed by Darcy and Elizabeth, although Bingley's character is still ostensibly the principal subject. In this way, comic incongruity gives way to emotional incongruity; the comedy of judgment openly and tacitly enacted by the characters becomes more highly charged and more complex; and the reader must register these judgments while adjusting his own.

Bingley assists the shift in subject to Darcy's character. His reply to Elizabeth begins genially and amusingly enough with, "I am exceedingly gratified . . . by your converting what my friend says into a compliment on the sweetness of my temper. But I am afraid you are giving it a turn which that gentleman did by no means intend." Sweet-tempered as he certainly is, Bingley now displays some of the strain which always attends being oneself a topic of conversation by inaccurately claiming that Darcy "would certainly think the better of me, if under such a circumstance I were to give a flat denial, and ride off as fast as I could." Elizabeth's reply perversely but wittily places the worst possible construction on this joke. "Would Mr. Darcy then consider the rashness of your original intention as atoned for by your obstinacy in adhering to it?" Bingley refers her to Darcy for an answer, and Darcy rightly observes that "You expect me to account for opinions which you chuse to call mine, but which I have never acknowledged." Whatever the reader's delight in Elizabeth's wit, he ought to recognize her peverseness and her injustice, both of which increase as her debate with Darcy continues; Darcy's increasing (and pardonable) irritation is evident, of course, both to the reader and to all the characters present.

Elizabeth at first refuses to argue the question Darcy raises. She wilfully prefers to make pointed remarks about his character: "To yield readily—easily—to the *persuasion* of a friend is no merit with you." Darcy ignores her attack and her change of subject. He attempts to continue the discussion as if it were rational and candid: "To yield without conviction is no compliment to the understanding of either." Elizabeth's reply constitutes her strongest criticism of Darcy in this scene and, in manner typical of Austen's highest comedy, reflects upon her rather than him: "You appear to me, Mr. Darcy, to allow nothing for the influence of friendship and affection." Elizabeth herself has been allowing nothing for the friendship and affection of Bingley and Darcy in her response to their dialogue. Instead, every speech of both has been even more "exactly in unison with her opinion of each" than were the initial exchanges between Miss Bingley and Darcy. At this point the reader must dissociate himself from Elizabeth's prejudice. Her misreading of the dialogue is wilful, and her attacks on Darcy are gratuitous. She is not the judge she thinks herself. The reader does not feel these incongruities as comic ones, however. The emotional undertones have become too serious, sharp, and powerful. Dialogue registers emotional incongruity rather than comic incongruity whenever the more or less intense emotional undercurrents which often lie beneath the surface of polite, witty talk are felt, to an extent by the characters themselves, and to a greater degree by the reader. The increasingly stilted dialogue testifies that Elizabeth and Darcy sense these emotional tensions. Their argument has become a conflict of wills, judgments, and feelings; Bingley registers the reader's discomfort as well as his own when he interrupts them.

The apparent subject of Elizabeth's and Darcy's dispute—openness to persuasion in general and Bingley's in particular—is not a central issue in the novel but does become important later in the action, when Bingley is persuaded by

Darcy that Jane does not love him and that he should leave Netherfield. Linear irony controls every speech in this scene, but its effects on this dispute are particularly complicated. Darcy will offer Bingley more than "one argument in favour of [the] propriety" of staying away from Netherfield and forgetting Jane, as his letter to Elizabeth explains, but only the "assurance . . . of your sister's indifference" (hardly an argument) convinces Bingley that he should remain in London. The humility in Bingley which Elizabeth praises in chapter 10 becomes his "great natural modesty, with a stronger dependence on [Darcy's] judgment than on his own," and allows him to be too easily persuaded. Finally, Elizabeth claims very complacently in chapter 10 that she is "not particularly speaking of such a case as you have supposed about Mr. Bingley. We may as well wait, perhaps, till the circumstance occurs, before we discuss the discretion of his behaviour thereupon." When the circumstance of Bingley's leaving Netherfield does occur, however, it is no matter for rational argument. Darcy's interference ruins Jane's happiness, and Elizabeth's angry reference to it when Darcy proposes precludes any discussion of Bingley's discretion.

Bingley's interruption of Elizabeth's exchange with Darcy brings the discussion to a close, for the moment. His discomfort at their quarrel also elicits from him an even more personal remark about Darcy than any of those Elizabeth has been guilty of: "I declare I do not know a more aweful object than Darcy, on particular occasions, and in particular places; at his own house especially, and of a Sunday evening when he has nothing to do." Elizabeth is considerate enough to check a laugh at this reflection on Darcy because she "thought she could perceive that he was rather offended," despite his smile. The reader is well aware that Darcy's offence is more likely to have proceeded from Elizabeth's remarks than from Bingley's. This dialogue then closes quietly. Darcy acknowledges Bingley's discomfort and his strategy by suggesting that Bingley wishes to "silence" the argument. Bingley agrees, still under the impression that the argument is about him ("If you and Miss Bennet will defer [your dispute] till I am out of the room, I shall be very thankful; and then you may say whatever you like of me"). Elizabeth is quite ready to desist. And Darcy resumes his letter, closing the scene with perfect symmetry.

Extended analysis makes this scene appear more solemn than it is. Austen's touch is light and sure, allowing comic incongruity to modulate brilliantly into a complex clash of wills, judgments, and feelings, closing in symmetry but not harmony, each character certain he understands what has passed and confirmed in his original opinion of the others despite all counterevidence offered within this "curious dialogue." The counterevidence is twofold: Elizabeth, Bingley, and Darcy reveal their own characters while they discuss Bingley's, Darcy's, and character in general. Discussion of character becomes a common topic in *Pride and Prejudice*, and frequently the character is present, as in this instance, to bear a part in the debate. In chapter 10, all three debaters observe the drama as well as participate in it, so that they are judging and responding to each other's characters, just as the reader must. As a result, the reader is asked to be aware of a threefold process of judgment when he reads the dialogue. On the surface the characters are openly judging Bingley's character. Tacitly, they are judging each other. And finally, the reader is judging them. As one critic says of *Emma*, "the process of reading runs parallel to the life read about." This process is only intensified when Darcy and Elizabeth discuss Darcy's character, pretending that Bingley's character is their subject. The reader must also register all the other elements in the dialogue: play of wit; talk on other important issues (character in general, persuasion, humility, pride); and comic and emotional incongruity acted out on qualities other than judgment (Miss Bingley's interest in Darcy, Darcy's and Bingley's friendship, Elizabeth's hostility to it). The technique of linear irony, variously implemented, requires further that the reader recall and reestimate the scene at various points later in the novel. These requirements alone are quite sufficiently exacting. Added to them is the complex awareness of three processes of judgment, required by Austen's discovery that the characters can talk about judgment while enacting it.

The differences between a scene like this and one in which the topic of conversation is less charged, however, thematic it may be, cannot be overemphasized. The debate on pride in chapter 5 is apposite. In *Pride and Prejudice*, Austen can be seen in the process of discovering the technique of dialogue she exploits so successfully afterward, the technique of choosing topics for conversation which do not simply reveal differences among characters but which voice, dramatize, and complicate the problems of judgment and sympathy which are the themes of the novels. This technique creates cumulative comic and emotional effects. Linear irony does permit these effects to be felt cumulatively in *Pride and Prejudice*, but in *Emma* and *Mansfield Park*, every speech and incident reflects back and forth upon every other. A web is created, not merely a line.

Another related and new technique is Austen's discovery that earlier discussions can be referred to and built upon in subsequent dialogues. This is a deceptively simple and obvious device, which only a great artist like Austen can use to advantage. It gives dialogue greater significance as well as verisimilitude. Characters do refer to previous conversations in the earlier novels, but their references serve different purposes. When Colonel Brandon exposes Willoughby's character to Elinor in *Sense and Sensibility*, he begins by asking her to recall an earlier conversation "in which I alluded to a lady I had once known, as resembling, in some measure, your sister Marianne." This lady was the near relation whom he had loved and lost, and whose illegitimate child had been seduced by

Willoughby. But Colonel Brandon's early allusion to the lady is simply meant to prepare the reader for the later revelation. Austen prescribes just such preparation in advice to a niece who is writing a novel. "St. Julian's History was quite a surprise to me; You had not very long known it yourself I suspect," she observes; "Had not you better give some hint of St. Julian's early history in the beginning of the story?" In *Pride and Prejudice*, however, references to earlier conversations help to create two significant new effects: a sense of interconnection between the dialogues which grants them a cumulative effect; and a sense that what is said by the characters is as important as what they do or experience.

A few critics have, like Norman Page, noted that *Pride and Prejudice* is "to an appreciable extent, not so much about what is done as about what is said." Others have noted that the conversations bear a close relation to the structure and themes. But these critics tend to focus on the linear irony which the dialogues create, or on analysis of the characters' styles of speech. Certainly these repay analysis; but the most important technical discoveries for increasing the weight and the significance of dialogue in this novel are even more simple and direct. One of Austen's most significant discoveries is that without violating decorum, surprisingly direct statements, either about emotions or revealing them, can be made; that these statements produce a much higher emotional temperature than most comedy permits; but that these powerful emotions can still be contained within a comedy of misjudgment and error.

The dialogues in the three later novels (properly, conversations) from one of Austen's most powerful devices to engage and control her readers' responses, for she becomes increasingly skilful in rendering the conscious and unconscious complexities of feeling which the clever and civilized conversation of a roomful of people will partially convey and partially conceal. She seems to have attempted such a scene in *Sense and Sensibility*, when Elinor and Marianne dine at Mrs. John Dashwood's London residence and meet Edward Ferrars's mother. Mrs. Ferrars and Mrs. John Dashwood slight Elinor and flatter Lucy Steele, ignorant of Lucy's engagement to Edward and fearing that Edward and Elinor are lovers. Though all the characters are completely at odds, full of misconceptions and of incompatible feelings and designs, the scene is not particularly moving or effective, for it is isolated. Emotional incongruity is best felt only as a cumulative effect. To orchestrate dialogues or conversations so that they are not isolated is a formidable achievement, and one which helps define the greatness of *Mansfield Park* and *Emma*. Austen acquires there the capacity to organize the feelings and judgments of more than two characters at once, whereas in *Pride and Prejudice* she does not really attempt to extend this exacting treatment of dialogue beyond the encounters of Elizabeth and Darcy, beginning at Netherfield and continuing to Darcy's second proposal.

Pride and Prejudice does approach *Emma* in density and power at the end, in the dialogues of Elizabeth and Darcy once they are engaged. Until then, their encounters are governed by some misconception about each other. An extreme of emotional incongruity is provided by Darcy's first proposal, for example, although the dialogue does register the cross-purposes in manners, motives, and judgments which usually produce the principally comic incongruities of the drawing-room scenes at Netherfield and Rosings. The emotional content of this scene precludes comedy, however. The dialogue demands complicated, even contradictory responses in feeling and judgment from the reader. When Darcy first proposes, readers must rejoice in the criticisms he receives, for he richly deserves them, yet because his love for Elizabeth also endears him to the reader, her humiliating rejection is painful. Sympathy and judgment, pain and pleasure, are evoked together and reinforce each other, producing in the reader an intensity and complexity of feeling which approach Elizabeth's own at the end of the scene.

Once Elizabeth and Darcy are engaged, they are free to discuss, compare, and reinterpret everything that has happened between them—particularly the original progress of their love. These last exchanges constitute the final stage of dialogue evident in the novel and create an entirely new effect. Ambiguity is dispelled and release and intimacy effected, to a degree equalled only at the end of *Emma* and touched on at the end of *Persuasion*. This release is an achievement so peculiar to Austen's novels that calling it a "stage" of dialogue is almost an indignity: it is rather a triumph of dialogue, something even Austen does not always accomplish, as *Persuasion* shows, but which no earlier novelist begins to approach. The triumph lies in actually rendering through conversation a relationship which wholly convinces and satisfies the imagination, the mind, and the heart, that a "happy ending" (the most hackneyed of literary conventions, yet the least common in serious art) has been not merely asserted or conjured up, but actually achieved.

At the end of *Pride and Prejudice*, literary convention and social convention unite in a marriage which fulfils all the demands of imagination and of personality: mutual affection and intimacy. Intimacy or knowledge produces an acceptance which goes beyond judgment (and all former misjudgments) to affection. In the light of affection, even Darcy's unpreparedness to laugh at himself is an amiable blemish, sure to disappear in Elizabeth's company. In Austen's work, the comedy of manners (including the social and literary conventions which govern it, and the dialogue and conversations which shape it) increasingly allows the fullest expression and development of character, for her comedy is successful and expressive in direct proportion to her mastery of convention, especially dialogue. In *Pride and Prejudice*, the final conversations of Elizabeth and Darcy ratify their intended marriage. This marriage affirms a literary and social convention which gives to judgment and sympathy their most solid, stable, and indeed highest form — affection and intimacy — and confirms that in life and in literature conventions need not be limitations: they are a resource, not a restraint, for the human spirit.

Chronology

1775 Jane Austen is born December 16 in the village of Steventon, Hampshire, to George Austen, parish clergyman, and Cassandra Leigh Austen. She is the seventh of eight children. She and her sister Cassandra are educated at Oxford and Southampton by the widow of a Principal of Brasenose College, then attend the Abbey School at Reading. Jane's formal education ends when she is nine years old.

1787–93 Austen writes various pieces for the amusement of her family (now collected in the three volumes of *Juvenilia*), the most famous of which is *Love and Freindship*. She and her family also perform various plays and farces in the family barn, some of which are written by Jane.

1793–95 Austen writes her first novel, the epistolary *Lady Susan*, and begins the epistolary *Elinor and Marianne*, which will become *Sense and Sensibility*.

1796–97 Austen completes *First Impressions*, an early version of *Pride and Prejudice*. Her father tries to get it published without success. Austen begins *Sense and Sensibility* and *Northanger Abbey*.

1798 Austen finishes a version of *Northanger Abbey*.

1801 George Austen retires to Bath with his family.

1801–2 Jane Austen probably suffers from an unhappy love affair (the man in question is believed to have died suddenly), and probably becomes engaged for a day to Harris Bigg-Wither.

1803 Austen sells a two-volume manuscript entitled *Susan* to a publisher for £10. It is advertised but never printed. This is a version of *Northanger Abbey*, probably later revised.

1803–5 Austen writes ten chapters of *The Watsons*, which is never finished.

1805 George Austen dies. Jane abandons work on *The Watsons*.

1805–6 Jane Austen, her mother, and her sister live in various lodgings in Bath.

1806–9   The three Austen women move to Southampton and live near one of Jane's brothers.

1809   The three Austen women move to Chawton Cottage, in Hampshire, which is part of the estate of Jane's brother Edward Austen (later Knight) who has been adopted by Thomas Knight, a relative. Edward has just lost his wife, who died giving birth to her tenth child, and the household has been taken over by Jane's favorite niece, Fanny.

1811   Austen decides to publish *Sense and Sensibility* anonymously at her own expense. It comes out in November in three volumes.

1811–12   Austen is probably revising *First Impressions* extensively, and beginning *Mansfield Park*.

1813   *Pride and Prejudice: A Novel. In Three Volumes. By the Author of 'Sense and Sensibility'* is published in January. Second editions of both books come out in November.

1814   *Mansfield Park* is published, again anonymously, and in three volumes. It sells out by November. Austen begins *Emma*.

1815   Austen finishes *Emma*, and begins *Persuasion*. Three volumes of *Emma* are published anonymously by a new publisher in December.

1816   A second edition of *Mansfield Park* is published.

1817   A third edition of *Pride and Prejudice* is published. Austen begins *Sanditon*. She moves to Winchester, where she dies after a year-long illness on July 18. She is buried in Winchester Cathedral. After her death, her family destroys much of her correspondence to protect her reputation.

1818   *Persuasion* and *Northanger Abbey* published posthumously together; their authorship is still officially anonymous.

Contributors

HAROLD BLOOM, Sterling Professor of the Humanities at Yale University, is the author of *The Anxiety of Influence*, *Poetry and Repression*, and many other volumes of literary criticism. His forthcoming study, *Freud: Transference and Authority*, attempts a full-scale reading of all of Freud's major writings. A MacArthur Prize Fellow, he is general editor of five series of literary criticism published by Chelsea House.

JANE NARDIN is Assistant Professor of English at the University of Wisconsin at Milwaukee. She is the author of *Those Elegant Decorums*, a study of Jane Austen.

STUART M. TAVE is William Rainey Harper Professor in the College and Professor of English at the University of Chicago. His books include *Some Words of Jane Austen*, *New Essays by De Quincey*, and a study of comic theory and criticism in the eighteenth and nineteenth centuries.

JULIET MCMASTER is Professor of English at the University of Alberta. She is the author of *Thackeray: The Major Novels*, *Trollope's Palliser Novels: Theme and Pattern*, and *Jane Austen on Love*.

GENE W. RUOFF is Associate Professor of English at the University of Illinois at Chicago. He has published several articles on Jane Austen.

JULIA PREWITT BROWN is the author of *Jane Austen's Novels: Social Change and Literary Form*.

DAVID MONAGHAN is Professor of English at Mount Saint Vincent University in Halifax, Nova Scotia. He is the editor of *Jane Austen in a Social Context* and the author of *Jane Austen: Structure and Social Vision* and *The Novels of John le Carré*.

SUSAN MORGAN is Assistant Professor of English at Stanford University. She is the author of *In the Meantime: Character and Perception in Jane Austen's Fiction*.

JAN FERGUS is Assistant Professor of English at Lehigh University and the author of *Jane Austen and the Didactic Novel*.

Bibliography

Armstrong, Nancy. "Inside Greimas's Square: Literary Characters and Cultural Constraints." In *The Sign in Music and Literature*, edited by Wendy Steiner, 52–66. Austin: University of Texas Press, 1981.

Babb, Howard. *Jane Austen's Novels: The Fabric of Dialogue*. Columbus: Ohio State University Press, 1962.

Barfoot, C. C. "Choice Against Fate in *Sense and Sensibility* and *Pride and Prejudice*." *Dutch Quarterly Review of Anglo-American Letters* 10 (1980): 176–98.

Berger, Carole. "The Rake and the Reader in Jane Austen's Novels." *Studies in English Literature 1500–1900* 15 (1975): 531–44.

Bloom, Harold, ed. *Modern Critical Views: Jane Austen*. New Haven: Chelsea House, 1986.

Boles, Carolyn G. "Jane Austen and the Reader: Rhetorical Techniques in *Northanger Abbey, Pride and Prejudice*, and *Emma*." *Emporia State Research Studies*, 30, no. 1 (1981): 152–67.

Bowen, Elizabeth. "Jane Austen." In *The English Novelists*, edited by Derek Verschoyle, 101–13. New York: Harcourt, Brace, 1936.

Bradbrook, Frank. *Jane Austen and Her Predecessors*. Cambridge: Cambridge University Press, 1967.

Brown, Julia Prewitt. *Jane Austen's Novels: Social Change and Literary Form*. Cambridge: Harvard University Press, 1979.

Brown, Lloyd. *Bits of Ivory: Narrative Techniques in Jane Austen's Fiction*. Baton Rouge: Louisiana State University Press, 1973.

Burgan, Mary H. "Mr. Bennet and the Failures of Fatherhood in Jane Austen's Novels." *Journal of English and Germanic Philology* 74 (1975): 536–52.

Burrows, J. F. "A Measure of Excellence: Modes of Comparison in *Pride and Prejudice*." *Sydney Studies in English* 5 (1979–80): 38–59.

Bush, Douglas. *Jane Austen*. New York: Macmillan, 1975.

Butler, Marilyn. *Jane Austen and the War of Ideas*. Oxford: Oxford University Press, 1975.

Cecil, David. *A Portrait of Jane Austen*. New York: Hill & Wang, 1980.

Chabot, C. Barry. "Jane Austen's Novels: The Vicissitudes of Desire." *American Imago* 32 (1975): 288–308.

Chapman, R. W. *Jane Austen: Facts and Problems*. Oxford: Clarendon Press, 1948.

Colby, R. A. *Fiction with a Purpose*. Bloomington: Indiana University Press, 1967.

Craik, W. A. *Jane Austen: The Six Novels*. London: Methuen, 1966.

DeRose, Peter. "Marriage and Self-Knowledge in *Emma* and *Pride and Prejudice*." *Renascence* 30 (1978): 199–216.

Devlin, David. *Jane Austen and Education*. New York: Barnes & Noble, 1975.

Donovan, Robert. *The Shaping Vision: Imagination in the English Novel from Defoe to Dickens*. Ithaca: Cornell University Press, 1966.

Duckworth, Alistair. *The Improvement of the Estate: A Study of Jane Austen's Novels*. Baltimore: Johns Hopkins University Press, 1971.

Duffy, Joseph M., Jr. "The Politics of Love: Marriage and the Good Society in *Pride and Prejudice*." *The University of Windsor Review* 11, no. 2 (1976): 5–26.

Fergus, Jan. *Jane Austen and the Didactic Novel:* Northanger Abbey, Sense and Sensibility, *and* Pride and Prejudice. Totowa, N. J.: Barnes & Noble, 1983.

Frazer, June M. "Stylistic Categories of Narrative in Jane Austen." *Style* 17, no. 1 (1983): 16–26.

Gilbert, Sandra M., and Susan Gubar. *The Madwoman in the Attic: The Woman Writer and the Nineteenth-Century Literary Imagination*. New Haven: Yale University Press, 1979.

Gillie, Christopher. *A Preface to Jane Austen*. London: Longmans, Green, 1975.

Giuffre, Giula. "The Ethical Mode of *Pride and Prejudice*." *Sydney Studies in English* 6 (1980–81): 17–29.

Halperin, John. *The Life of Jane Austen*. Sussex, England: Harvester Press, 1984.

———, ed. *Jane Austen: Bicentenary Essays*. Cambridge: Cambridge University Press, 1975.

Hardy, Barbara. *A Reading of Jane Austen*. New York: New York University Press, 1976.

Hardy, John. *Jane Austen's Heroines: Intimacy in Human Relationships*. London: Routledge & Kegan Paul, 1984.

Heath, William, ed. *Discussions of Jane Austen*. Boston: D. C. Heath, 1961.

Kelly, G. "The Art of Reading in *Pride and Prejudice*." *English Studies in Canada* 10, no. 2 (1984): 156–71.

Kennard, Jean E. *Victims of Convention*. Hamden, Conn.: Archon, 1978.

Kestner, Joseph A., III. *Jane Austen: Spatial Structure and Thematic Variations*. Saltzburg:

Institut für Englischen Sprache und Literatur, University of Saltzburg, 1974.

Kirkham, Margaret. *Jane Austen: Feminism and Fiction*. Totowa, N. J.: Barnes & Noble, 1983.

Kroeber, Karl. *Styles in Fictional Structure: The Art of Jane Austen, Charlotte Brontë, George Eliot*. Princeton: Princeton University Press, 1971.

Lascelles, Mary. *Jane Austen and Her Art*. Oxford: Oxford University Press, 1939.

Lerner, Laurence. *The Truthtellers: Jane Austen, George Eliot, D. H. Lawrence*. New York: Schocken, 1967.

Liddell, Robert. *Novels of Jane Austen*. London: Longmans, Green, 1963.

Litz, A. Walton. *Jane Austen: A Study of Her Artistic Development*. New York: Oxford University Press, 1965.

McKeon, Richard. "*Pride and Prejudice*: Thought, Character, Argument, and Plot." *Critical Inquiry* 5 (1979): 511–27.

McMaster, Juliet. *Jane Austen on Love*. Victoria, B.C.: University of Victoria, 1978.

———, ed. *Jane Austen's Achievement*. London: Macmillan, 1976.

Mansell, Darrel. *The Novels of Jane Austen: An Interpretation*. London: Macmillan, 1973.

Mews, Hazel. *Frail Vessels: Woman's Role in Women's Novels from Fanny Burney to George Eliot*. London: Athlone, 1969.

Moler, Kenneth L. *Jane Austen's Art of Illusion*. Lincoln: University of Nebraska Press, 1968.

Monaghan, David, ed. *Jane Austen in a Social Context*. London: Macmillan, 1981.

Mudrick, Marvin. *Jane Austen: Irony as Defense and Discovery*. Princeton: Princeton University Press, 1952.

Newton, Judith Lowder. *Women, Power, and Subversion: Social Strategies in British Fiction, 1778–1860*. Athens: University of Georgia Press, 1981.

Nineteenth-Century Fiction 30, no. 3 (December 1975). Special Jane Austen issue.

Odmark, John. *An Understanding of Jane Austen's Novels*. Oxford: Basil Blackwell, 1972.

O'Neill, Judith. *Critics on Jane Austen*. Miami, Fla.: University of Miami Press, 1970.

Page, Norman. *The Language of Jane Austen*. Oxford: Basil Blackwell, 1972.

Paris, Bernard. *Character and Conflict in Jane Austen's Novels*. Detroit: Wayne State University Press, 1979.

Persuasions: Journal of the Jane Austen Society of North America, 1979–.

Phillips, K. C. *Jane Austen's English*. London: Andre Deutsch, 1970.

Piggott, Patrick. *The Innocent Diversion: A Study of Music in the Life and Writings of Jane Austen*. London: Douglas Cleverdon, 1979.

Polhemus, Robert. *Comic Faith: The Great Tradition from Austen to Joyce*. Chicago: University of Chicago Press, 1980.

Poovey, Mary. *The Proper Lady and the Woman Writer: Ideology as Style in the Works of Mary Wollstonecraft, Mary Shelley, and Jane Austen*. Chicago: University of Chicago Press, 1984.

Rees, Joan. *Jane Austen: Woman and Writer*. New York: St. Martin's, 1976.

Roberts, Warren. *Jane Austen and the French Revolution*. New York: St. Martin's, 1979.

Roth, Barry, and Joel Weinsheimer, eds. *An Annotated Bibliography of Jane Austen Studies, 1952–1972*. Charlottesville: University Press of Virginia, 1973.

Rubinstein, E., ed. *Twentieth-Century Interpretations of* Pride and Prejudice: *A Collection of Critical Essays*. Englewood Cliffs, N. J.: Prentice-Hall, 1969.

Scott, P. J. M. *Jane Austen: A Reassessment*. Totowa, N. J.: Barnes & Noble, 1982.

Sherry, James. "*Pride and Prejudice*: The Limits of Society." *Studies in English Literature 1500–1900* 19, no. 4 (1979): 609–22.

Sherry, Norman. *Jane Austen*. London: Evans Brothers, 1966.

Siefert, Susan. *The Dilemma of the Talented Heroine: A Study in Nineteenth-Century Fiction*. Montreal: Eden Press, 1977.

Smith, LeRoy W. *Jane Austen and the Drama of Woman*. London: Macmillan, 1983.

Southam, B. C. *Jane Austen*. Essex: Longman Group, 1975.

_____, ed. *Critical Essays on Jane Austen*. London: Routledge & Kegan Paul, 1968.

_____, ed. *Jane Austen: The Critical Heritage*. London: Routledge & Kegan Paul, 1968.

Steeves, Harrison. *Before Jane Austen*. New York: Holt, Rinehart & Winston, 1965.

Studies in the Novel 7, no. 1 (1975). Special Jane Austen issue.

Tanner, Tony. *Jane Austen*. Cambridge: Harvard University Press, 1986.

Ten Harmsel, Henrietta. *Jane Austen: A Study in Fictional Conventions*. The Hague: Mouton, 1964.

Todd, Janet, ed. *Jane Austen: New Perspectives. Women & Literature* n.s. 3. New York: Holmes & Meier, 1983.

Wallace, Robert K. *Jane Austen and Mozart: Classical Equilibrium in Fiction and Music*. Athens: University of Georgia Press, 1983.

Watt, Ian. *Jane Austen: A Collection of Critical Essays*. Englewood Cliffs, N. J.: Prentice-Hall, 1963.

Weinsheimer, Joel, ed. *Jane Austen Today*. Athens: University of Georgia Press, 1975.

Welty, Eudora. "A Note on Jane Austen." *Shenandoah* 20, no. 3 (1969): 3–17.

Wiesenfarth, Joseph. *The Errand of Form*. New York: Fordham University Press, 1967.

Williams, Raymond. *The Country and the City*. New York: Oxford University Press, 1973.

Willis, Lesley H. "Eyes and the Imagery of Sight in *Pride and Prejudice*." *English Studies in Canada* 2, no. 2 (1976): 156–62.

Wilson, Mona. *Jane Austen and Some Contemporaries*. London: Cresset Press, 1938.

Wilt, Judith. "Jane Austen's Men: Inside/Outside 'the Mystery.'" *Women & Literature* 2 (1982): 59–76.

The Wordsworth Circle 7, no. 4 (1976). Special Jane Austen issue.

Wright, Andrew. *Jane Austen's Novels: A Study in Structure*. New York: Oxford University Press, 1953.

Acknowledgments

"Propriety as a Test of Character: *Pride and Prejudice*" by Jane Nardin from *Those Elegant Decorums: The Concept of Propriety in Jane Austen's Novels* by Jane Nardin, © 1973 by the State University of New York. Reprinted by permission.

"Affection and the Amiable Man" (originally entitled "Affection and the Mortification of Elizabeth Bennet") by Stuart M. Tave from *Some Words of Jane Austen* by Stuart M. Tave, © 1973 by the University of Chicago. Reprinted by permission of the University of Chicago Press.

"Love and Pedagogy: Austen's Beatrice and Benedick" (originally entitled "Love and Pedagogy") by Juliet McMaster from *Jane Austen on Love (English Literary Studies no. 13)* by Juliet McMaster, © 1978 by Juliet McMaster. Reprinted by permission of the author and of the editor of *English Literary Studies*, University of Victoria. This essay originally appeared in *Jane Austen Today*, edited by Joel Weinsheimer, University of Georgia Press, 1975.

"The Dramatic Dilemma" (originally entitled "The Sense of a Beginning: *Mansfield Park* and Romantic Narrative") by Gene W. Ruoff from *The Wordsworth Circle* 10, no. 1 (Winter 1979), © 1979 By Marilyn Guall. Reprinted by permission of the author and of Marilyn Guall, editor of *The Wordsworth Circle*.

"Authorial Voice and the Total Perspective" (originally entitled "Necessary Conjunctions: *Pride and Prejudice*") by Julia Prewitt Brown from *Jane Austen's Novels: Social Change and Literary Form* by Julia Prewitt Brown, © 1979 by the President and Fellows of Harvard College. Reprinted by permission of Harvard University Press

"*Pride and Prejudice*: Structure and Social Vision" (originally entitled "*Pride and Prejudice*") by David Monaghan from *Jane Austen: Structure and Social Vision* by David Monaghan, © 1980 by David Monaghan. Reprinted by permission of the author, Macmillan Press Ltd., and Barnes & Noble Books, Totowa, New Jersey.

"Intelligence in *Pride and Prejudice*" by Susan Morgan from *In the Meantime: Character and Perception in Jane Austen's Fiction* by Susan Morgan, © 1980 by the University of Chicago. Reprinted by permission of the University of Chicago Press.

"The Comedy of Manners" (originally entitled "*Pride and Prejudice*") by Jan Fergus from *Jane Austen and the Didactic Novel:* Northanger Abby, Sense and Sensibility, *and* Pride and Prejudice by Jan Fergus, © 1983 by Jan Fergus. Reprinted by permission of Barnes & Noble Books, Totowa, New Jersey, and Macmillan Press Ltd.

Index

Affection, 21; and gratitude, 37; and marriage, 31–38, 71, 126

Agreeableness: and amiability, 21, 23, 30; in works of Jane Austen, 24–25

Amiability: and agreeableness, 21, 23, 30; in works of Jane Austen, 21–38; in eighteenth-century fiction, 22; and marriage, 25–26; and pride, 3–5

Archer, Isabel (*The Portrait of a Lady*), 98, 102

Austen, Anna, 23, 109, 124

Austen, Cassandra, 23

Austen, Jane: and Anna Austen, 23, 109, 124; on amiability, 21–38; and Charlotte Brontë, 39, 40, 42; compared with Fanny Burney, 1, 107–8; classicism of, 50; compliments in works of, 109, 111; courtship in works of, 59–60, 62–83, 103; critical views of, 86–87; dancing in works of, 62–73; passion for detail of, 14; use of dialogue of, 57, 114–26; as dramatist, 51; compared with George Eliot, 1, 55–56, 57; and Fanny Knight, 23–24, 34, 37; compared with Henry Fielding, 1–2, 57; flirtation in works of, 110–12; freedom in works of, 85, 88–89; on gratitude as motive for love, 88–90, 104; heroines of, 1, 2; humor of, 9, 113–14; influence of, on nineteenth-century novel, 39–41; intelligence in works of, 88–105; irony of, 1, 56–57; compared with Henry James, 57; compared with Ben Johnson, 1; juvenilia of, 22; on marriage, 31–38, 56; on

morality, 19; narrative voice of, 53–58; old maids in works of, 32, 35, 96; parent-child relationships in works of, 18, 35–36, 58; pedagogy in works of, 39–47; on *Pride and Prejudice*, 43, 88; Protestant sensibility of, 2; compared with Samuel Richardson, 1–2, 107–10, 112–14; on sensibility, 96; sexualilty in works of, 43; compared with William Shakespeare, 1; social comedy in works of, 107–8, 109 112–26; on society, 1, 62, 63, 83; and sense of structure, 113–14; technique of, 70–71, 74, 82, 90–93, 94, 117–18, 120, 123–26; and use of wit, 114–26. *Works:* Juvenilia, 22; *The Watsons,* 33. *See also Emma; Mansfield Park; Northanger Abbey; Persuasion; Pride and Prejudice, Sense and Sensibility*

Bates, Miss (*Emma*), 27, 32, 96, 107, 114

Bennet, Elizabeth, 49, 114; and affection, for Fitzwilliam Darcy, 31, 34–35, 36–38; on amiability, 23, 28–30; compared with Shakespeare's Beatrice, 42–43; and Jane Bennet, 34, 93, 94; and Lydia Bennet's marriage, 36; and Charles Bingley, 10, 43, 93, 99; character of, 60; and William Collins, 70, 71, 93, 94, 95; Darcy's courtship of, 50, 51, 59–83; compared with Elinor Dashwood, 7; detachment of, 89, 93–95, 99–102; freedom of, 85–86, 89; and gratitude to Darcy,